VIKINGS

Acknowledgements

Marjolein Stern: The summer in which this book was written was a very exciting, but busy, time for my family. I would like to thank them, especially Mattijs and Linnea, for their patience, enthusiasm and support. I would also like to thank Roderick for doing this project with me.

Roderick Dale: I would like to thank Karen for supporting and believing in me, and my mother for her unflagging support over the years. She would have been thrilled to see this book.

THIS IS AN ANDRE DEUTSCH BOOK

This edition published in 2016 by Andre Deutsch
An imprint of the Carlton Publishing Group
20 Mortimer Street
London W1T 3JW

First published in 2014

Design © Carlton Publishing Group 2014, 2016
Text © Marjolein Stern & Roderick Dale 2014, 2016

A CIP catalogue for this book is available from the British Library.

ISBN: 978-0-233-00494-5

Printed in China

The content in this book previously appeared in *The Viking Experience* in 2014

10 9 8 7 6 5 4 3 2 1

VIKINGS

RAIDS · CULTURE · LEGACY

MARJOLEIN STERN & RODERICK DALE

ANDRE DEUTSCH

CONTENTS

INTRODUCTION

In the late eighth century a reign of terror began in England, which would change aspects of English life forever. A group of three ships from Hordaland in Norway arrived at the coast near Dorchester in AD 789. The local reeve, or high official of the area, went to meet them, to persuade them to go up to the town, where he might question them about their reasons for coming there and record their presence, as the laws required. The Norwegians killed the reeve and his companions. What they did after that is not recorded, but the *Anglo-Saxon Chronicle* states that these were the first Norwegians to seek out the lands of the English people. This was a chilling warning of what was to come. Four years later, in AD 793, raiders descended on Lindisfarne and the Viking Age began in earnest. What followed was years of raiding, until the raiders started bringing their wives and children with them to settle the areas that previously they had plundered.

The people who did this were known to the Anglo-Saxons of England as Vikings. They were primarily Danes in the east of England and Norwegians in Scotland, Ireland, and the west of England. Danes and Norwegians plundered the coasts of Europe, besieging Paris in the ninth century and even going so far as to claim that they had sacked Rome. Some of these raids were written about in the Frankish annals or in the *Anglo-Saxon Chronicle*, others were recorded by Muslim and Byzantine chroniclers at the time they happened or shortly afterwards.

Swedish Vikings went east towards Byzantium, founding the Russian towns of Staraja Ladoga, Novgorod and Kiev as they travelled. Their actions were chronicled too by Ibn Fadlan (see page 34), who passed on to us the most complete description of a Viking funeral known, while other Arab chroniclers recorded their ferocity and the terror they inspired. Chroniclers recorded their deeds at the court of the Byzantine Empire, where Vikings were members of the feared Varangian Guard, the personal bodyguards of the Byzantine emperor (see page 28–34).

The origin of the term "Viking" has traditionally been thought to derive from the language of the Vikings, which is known as Old Norse. In Old Norse the word *vík* means an inlet or creek, and people that hid in inlets to ambush others were vikings. Research shows that the word is probably of Anglo-Frisian origin instead because there is no evidence of the Old Norse word *víking* before the tenth century. The Anglo-Saxon equivalent of *víking* already existed in the eighth century, which means it must have been borrowed by the Vikings from those they raided. In the language of the Anglo-Saxons – Old English – a *wīcing* was a pirate. This word probably comes from the Old English word *wīc*, meaning camp or fort. Thus Vikings were pirates who lived in camps or forts. This usage was transmitted into Old Norse, the language of the Vikings, and they very quickly started to use it to describe anyone who was a pirate or went on a raiding voyage. To the Scandinavian peoples, "viking" was a job description and was applied only to those who did this.

It was later that the term started being used to describe all Scandinavians. In the Victorian period, there was a lot of interest in Vikings and in Old Norse literature. This coincided with the rise of national romanticism and the creation of nation states. Authors like Sir Walter Scott used Old Norse literature as a tool to help create these national identities. The popularity of the Vikings flourished for the whole of the nineteenth century under the attention of the many authors who wrote about these noble seafarers. Although it had been adopted into modern English in only the early part of the nineteenth century, the word Viking was soon in common usage and had come to mean all Scandinavians of the Viking Age. We use the term "Viking" nowadays in the same way. Although technically wrong, it is a convenient shorthand for referring to people of Scandinavian origin between *c.* AD 800 and *c.* AD 1100.

Marjolein Stern & Roderick Dale

ABOVE The prow of the ninth-century Gokstad ship shortly after its excavation in 1880 (see page 32). Shields on the side of the ship have been put back in place, and the burial chamber has been reconstructed on the deck. This ship was the last resting place of a powerful man in his forties who had died in battle.

CHAPTER | ONE

ORIGINS OF THE SCANDINAVIAN NATIONS

THE VIKING ORIGIN MYTH

According to Snorri Sturluson, writing in the thirteenth century (see page 21), the origin of the Norse gods can be traced to a Trojan prince called Tror, grandson of King Priam. Tror's many times-great grandson was Woden, whom the Norse called Odin (see picture left). Odin had the gift of prophecy and knew that if he travelled to north west Europe he would be remembered for all time, so he set off with a large following. Odin stopped in Frankia where he fathered three sons, who were the origin of the Völsung dynasty, known to many from Wagner's *Ring Cycle.* Then he travelled to Denmark, where he established his son Skiöld as king and from him the Skiöldung dynasty, which we know from the Old English epic *Beowulf*, was descended. Odin then travelled to Sweden, where he established himself before moving on and setting up sons as rulers of Sweden and Norway. Thus, according to Scandinavian legend, all rulers in the north were descended from Odin, and, because of his success, Odin became revered as a god.

STONE AGE AND BRONZE AGE SCANDINAVIA

In reality, settlers in Scandinavia first arrived in the Stone Age, following the end of the last ice age. These settlers were nomadic hunter-gatherers, who followed the reindeer herds and exploited the resources of vast territorial areas up to approximately 100,000 square kilometres (39,000 square miles). They had reached southern Sweden by 14,000 years ago and, over the following 5,000 years, worked their way northwards, adapting their lifestyles to the coastal landscape in which they found themselves. From *c.* 8000 BC–6000 BC, the landscape of Scandinavia changed to resemble more the landscape we know today, as forests started to cover the tundra and the sea level rose. Around 4000 BC agricultural practices from central Europe began to be adopted, although they did not become important elements of the economy until *c.* 3100 BC. Space for farms was cleared by burning the vegetation, crops like wheat and barley began to be cultivated and domesticated animals were kept.

The Nordic Bronze Age (*c.* 1700 BC–500 BC) began rather later than the Bronze Age in the rest of Europe. The raw materials of bronze (tin and copper) were not available in Scandinavia and must have been imported from the south. The domesticated horse was also introduced to Scandinavia at this time, quickly becoming an important part of daily and religious life, as it continued to be in the Viking Age.

Evidence for trade with distant countries in the Bronze Age is present in the form of swords from Germany, Hungary and Romania, and miniature axes from the eastern Mediterranean or Bulgaria. Similarly, Scandinavian amber has been found as far afield as Mycenae and Pylos in Greece. This clearly shows that the Scandinavians did not live in isolation from the rest of Europe and that trade was an important part of life, as it was later too.

Ritual life is represented by finds like the Trundholm sun chariot (*c.* 1800 BC–1600 BC) , discovered in Denmark in 1902, which consists of a statue of a horse and a bronze disc to represent the sun, both mounted on a wheeled carriage. Examples of the lur, a type of curved bronze horn, have been found in Scandinavia and are also depicted in petroglyphs, rock carvings that show various aspects of Scandinavian life. Some of these petroglyphs are thought to include figures who are precursors of the gods depicted in Norse mythology.

HORNED HELMETS

Most people know that Vikings did not wear horned helmets, yet the myth persists and the image of a stout Norseman with horned helmet still appears in, among other things, advertising and cartoons. This image arose in the nineteenth century as part of Scandinavian romanticism and has been credited to Carl Doepler, who designed the costumes for the first production of Wagner's *Ring Cycle.* Before this time, and before the coining of the term "Viking Age" in 1876, horned helmets were the province of early Germanic warriors. They had been depicted with these helmets from at least the sixteenth century onwards, because early scholars assumed that descriptions of Celts wearing adorned helmets also included the Germanic tribes. So, when the Viking took centre stage in popular culture, he was quickly associated with the horned helmet, even though no examples of Viking Age helmets with horns have ever been found.

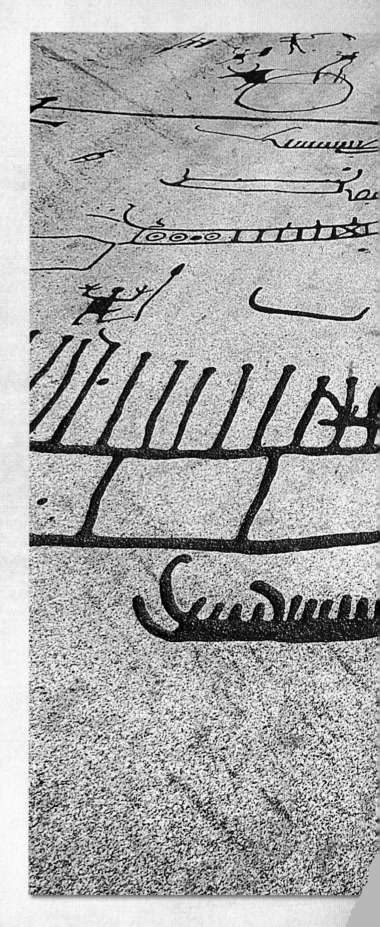

RIGHT Bronze Age rock carvings from Vitlycke, Sweden, of ships. Rowers are depicted kneeling in them as upright strokes. One ship in the centre has a crew that includes warriors blowing lur horns. The design of the ships is the same as that of the Iron Age Hjortspring boat.

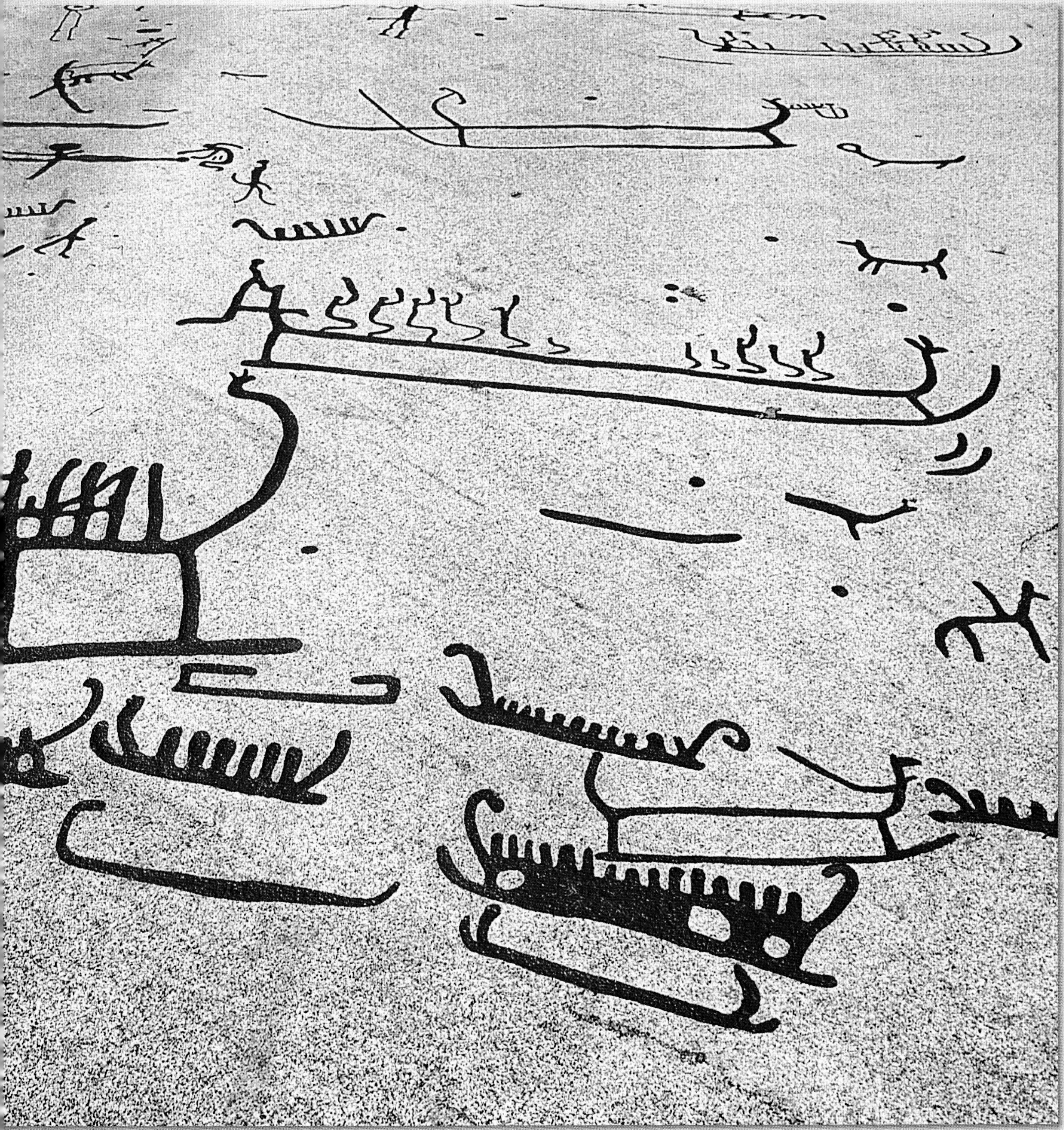

Horned helmets do exist, however. A Bronze Age statuette of a kneeling figure wearing a helmet with large curving horns on its sides was found at Grevensvænge in Denmark. Two helmets found at Viksø in Denmark, dating from *c.* 1000 BC, confirmed that horned helmets existed. Many of the Bronze Age petroglyphs also depict figures with horned helmets. It is probable that these helmets were not intended for use in combat but were worn for ceremonial or ritual occasions, because their functionality is severely impaired by the presence of the horns.

THE IRON AGE

The Iron Age in Scandinavia (*c.* 500 BC–AD 1100) extends from the Bronze Age until the end of the Viking Age. Before the Viking Age, it is generally

LEFT A helmet with horns dating from *c.* 1000 BC. It, and another like it, was found at Viksø, Denmark. The helmets were probably used in rituals rather than in battle, because they show no battle damage.

OPPOSITE An iron helmet decorated with bronze plaques. The helmet was found at Vendel, Sweden, and dates from the mid-sixth century. The plaques depict warriors fighting and may represent an initiation ritual that the wearer underwent.

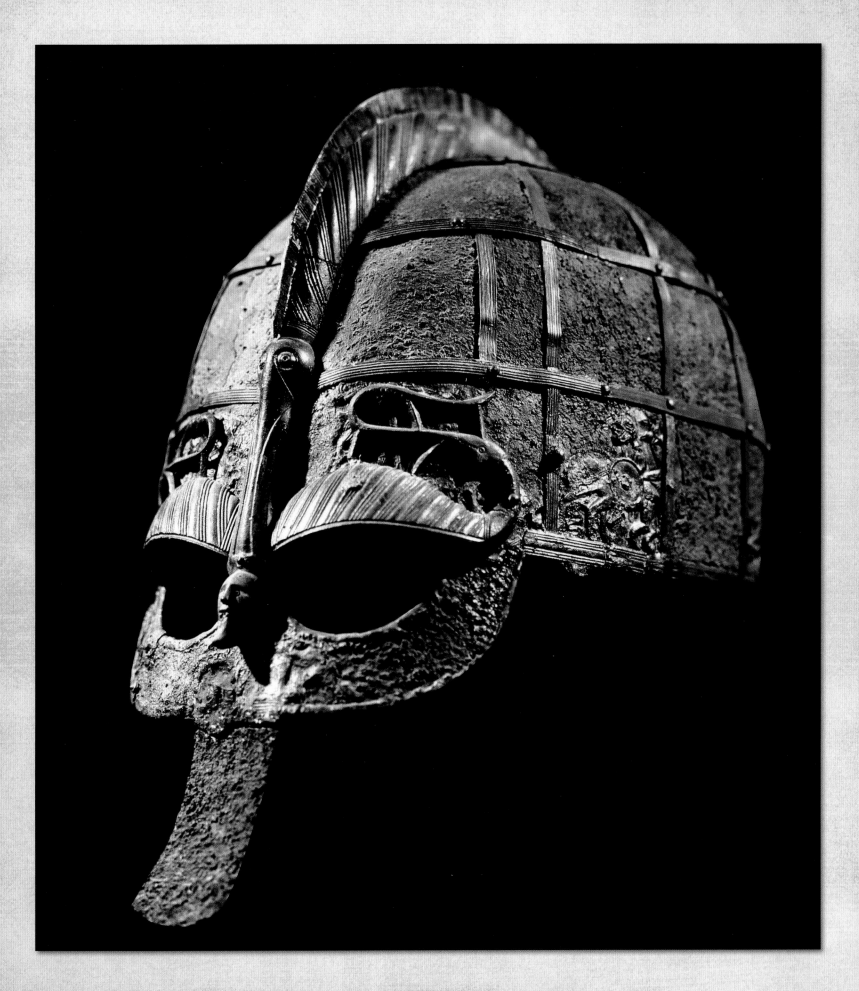

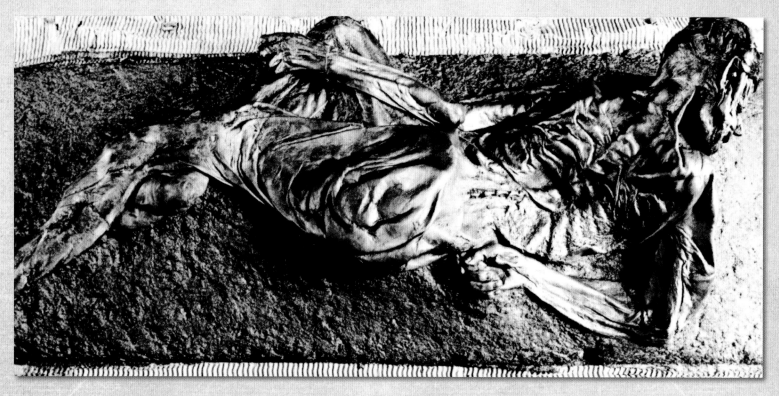

divided into three periods: the Pre-Roman Iron Age (500 BC–1 BC), the Roman Iron Age (1 BC–AD 400) and the Germanic Iron Age (AD 400–800). These divisions correspond to the relationship that Scandinavia had with the Roman Empire. The period is characterized by social change from more egalitarian tribal societies to the chiefdoms and petty kingdoms that would become medieval states as time progressed.

The Pre-Roman Iron Age shows great contrasts in different areas. In the north, in Finnmark, Norway, hunting and fishing were the primary means of subsistence, as had been the case for thousands of years. In the south – in Jutland, Denmark, for example – villages that were supported by agriculture and animal husbandry had grown up. Near these villages, field systems that consist of larger fields divided into smaller plots for individual farms have been found. As the period progressed, large areas of forest were cleared for new villages and farms, and the soil appears to have become exhausted, resulting in the abandonment of farms and villages.

Roman authors tell of a southward migration by Germanic peoples, leading to great battles with the Romans. It seems likely that this was in part a result of the poorer growing conditions and greater difficulty in feeding people.

During the Roman Iron Age, Scandinavia suddenly found itself on the border of the Roman Empire. The Empire officially ended at the Rhine, but the tribes to the north of it became Romanized and that culture was passed on northwards by them. The Romans sought alliances with the Scandinavians so that they could access the resources of the north. They also employed Germanic mercenaries to fight other barbarian tribes in Europe. Burials show that the result of this contact was an increase in the wealth of those at the top of the social tree. They were buried with expensive Roman artefacts as well as their own local goods, while other burials remained as poor as they had in earlier periods. This suggests that kingdoms were more fully emerging now under the leadership of these most wealthy and powerful people.

ABOVE The body of the Grauballe man from the third century BC, who was preserved in a peat bog near Grauballe, Denmark. His throat had been cut and he was buried naked in the bog.

OPPOSITE The face of Tollund Man, a body found preserved in a peat bog near Tollund, Denmark. He was killed in the fourth century BC and still had the noose that killed him around his neck.

ABOVE The Trundholm
Sun Chariot from
Denmark may have been
used as a calendar but is
probably also of religious
significance. It dates to
c. 1800 BC.

The Germanic Iron Age followed the fall of the Western Roman Empire, which resulted from the migrations of Germanic tribes. At the beginning of this period, the Anglo-Saxons had just established their kingdoms in England, while the Ostrogoths in Italy, the Visigoths in Spain and southern France, and the Franks in France and Germany were the strongest kingdoms in Europe. These kingdoms all claimed descent from Scandinavian tribes and their leaders claimed to be descended from the Germanic gods. Many medieval legendary Icelandic sagas describe events of this time, such as *Hrólfs saga kraka*, which contains characters that are also described in the Anglo-Saxon epic *Beowulf*. It was also in this period that the characteristic interlace decoration that is associated with Viking Age iconography developed.

This was an important time in which the conditions for the Viking Age were forged. The economic and political conflicts that developed towards the end of the Germanic Iron Age may have been the stimulus for the first Viking raids, as the differences between the Christian kingdoms to the south and the pagan Scandinavian kingdoms became greater.

HJORTSPRING AND IRON AGE WARFARE

The discovery at Hjortspring Mose in southern Jutland of a wooden plank boat from the Early Iron Age (*c.* 350 BC–300 BC) demonstrated the warlike nature of Iron Age Scandinavians. The boat contained many shields, shield bosses, iron spearheads, iron swords and the remains of several coats of mail. It was also found with wooden paddles that would have been used to propel the boat, wooden pots (*pyxides*) that may have contained war paint, a blacksmith's bellows and other everyday items. A horse, a dog, a lamb and a calf were included in the burial.

This area is now a peat bog, but would have been a small lake at the time of the burial. The find has been interpreted as a sacrifice involving the weapons and armour of a defeated invading warband. Analysis of the finds suggests that the warband would have consisted of about ten leaders, with swords, and 80–90 men, armed with spears. They would have been carried in four boats, including the one that was sacrificed in Hjortspring Mose.

The boat is of unusual design, with two up-curved spines joined by a stick at both prow and stern. These are purely decorative elements that have no functional use in the design of the boat. Its total length is approximately 21 metres (68 feet) from stem to stern. It is 2 metres (6 feet 6 inches) wide and weighs about 500 kilograms (1,100 pounds). It has space for 22 men inside, who would have propelled the boat with paddles. The design of this boat is similar to petroglyphs of boats from Scandinavia during the Bronze Age, suggesting that this was a common style of boat throughout that period and into the Iron Age. Like the later Viking ships, it was clinker-built – a method of boat-building using overlapping planks – and so may provide a clue to the origin of this design feature, which helped make Viking ships so versatile.

RIGHT Detail of a male face with curly hair and a moustache from the Early Iron Age Dejbjerg Wagon, which was sacrificed in a bog in West Jutland. The metal fittings all have male faces like this one.

OVERLEAF The Hjortspring boat was sacrificed in a bog together with a collection of weapons, armour and animals. It probably carried a crew of 22 men and was paddled rather than rowed.

CHAPTER | TWO

EXPLORATION

TRANSPORT

Some Vikings travelled extensively. Others remained at home on their farms, growing crops and fishing to survive, but they still needed to travel occasionally, perhaps to to visit a neighbour or to go to the *Althing*, the yearly assembly (see pages 68 and 91).

Horses were a common means of transport, particularly in Iceland, where travel was easier by land. Although the horses used were not large and were certainly not war horses like medieval knights used, they were a means of travelling relatively quickly. The Vikings made good use of this mobility in their forays abroad. When they invaded East Anglia in the ninth century, they promptly sought out stocks of horses so that they could more easily travel and raid with less danger of getting caught by the Saxon army.

Archaeological evidence in the form of fittings and tack for wagons, as well as rutted roads and tracks, shows that the Vikings used wagons. They were probably drawn either by horses or oxen, although the Norse god Thor is said to have driven a wagon pulled by goats, while the goddess Freyja had one that was drawn by cats. One particularly well-decorated wagon was buried with the ship found at the Oseberg farm in Norway. This is a four-wheeled wagon that was not actually fully functional; the design prevented the wheels from turning properly. Therefore it was probably built specifically for the funeral, but the construction techniques used are still valuable for understanding how wagons were built.

In the winter, the Vikings used skis to cross snow, skates made of bone to cross iced-over lakes or sledges drawn by horses to carry themselves and their goods or families.

Skis were wooden and the skier propelled himself along with a single stick, in a process that was much like punting nowadays, unlike modern techniques involving two ski poles. Sometimes the skier would carry a passenger on the back of the skis, too. One episode from Snorri Sturluson's history *Heimskringla* records that the Icelander Þoroddr Snorrason and his companion met a Norwegian called Arnljótr while on a tax-collecting expedition in Jamtaland early in the eleventh century. They were being pursued by enemies but were too slow on their skis, so Arnljótr got both of them to ride on the back of his skis and outdistanced their pursuers easily. Although fictionalized, this idea of carrying passengers may reflect actual practice.

Skates were made of bone. They had a broad, flat base, rather than the blades that we are used to now, and were attached to the shoes using leather thongs. The skater then propelled himself over the ice with a pole in the same manner as a skier.

The horses that drew sledges were shod with special spiked shoes to enable them to get traction in the poor going. The sledges could be quite simple in design, with up-curved runners, and resembling a modern wooden sledge, or might be highly decorated like the three from the Oseberg burial. These were intricately carved and had boxes on the main body that could have carried goods or a person. Ordinary sledges might also have been fitted with undecorated boxes for this purpose.

Boats and ships were a part of daily life in coastal areas. Some parts of Scandinavia were most easily accessible by boat, so travel to those areas was almost exclusively over water. Boats were used to go fishing, to cross waterways to visit other farms in the area, or to travel great distances for raiding and trading. There were a variety of different types of ship and the number of names for "ship" in Old Norse indicates how important they were. However, it is difficult to determine whether a particular word for a ship actually defines the type of ship it was, because many terms are poetical and others are used synonymously.

The *dreki* (dragon) was the famous longship, a sleek warship the sole purpose of which was to carry men into battle. It was also known as the *skeið* or *snekkja*. This ship could be rowed at speed as well as being powered by a large square sail. The mast could be unshipped easily when not needed, such as when passing under low bridges or when the Vikings wished to approach their

BELOW: Slate with sketch of Viking Ship, Shetland

A ninth-century sketch of a Viking Ship on slate, found at a farm on the Shetland Islands north of Scotland. Vikings began to settle permanently in the Shetland Islands from the ninth century onwards.

target stealthily. Examples of these ships are the Oseberg and Gokstad ships (see picture on page 20 and pages 30–31, 45 and 92), although their design suggests royal ships of state rather than actual warships. Ships 2 and 5 of the five found at Skuldelev in Denmark are more likely to have been used in battle. One of the most famous from literature was Olaf Tryggvason's own ship, *The Long Serpent*, which was said to be the largest warship ever built.

Cargo ships (*knörr* in Old Norse) were broader than warships and designed to carry larger loads, rather than a cargo of warriors. Their greater draught required deeper harbours. Examples of Viking Age cargo ships were recovered from the fjord at Skuldelev. Reconstructions of these have shown that they could be sailed by small crews of about six men and that they could carry up to 5,000 pounds (24 tons) of cargo, which indicates that they were trading in everyday goods and not just luxuries.

SEA ROUTES AND NAVIGATION TECHNIQUES

The Vikings are famous for their seafaring abilities. In part this is the result of the clinker-built ships that they used, which had a flexibility that other nations' ships did not have. This meant that the ships could flex with the waves and could be sailed in seas where less well constructed ships could not venture. Viking warships also had a shallow draught, which permitted them to sail right up onto beaches, thus enabling a form of amphibious landing.

Seafaring was also a significant part of the Vikings' own popular consciousness. Voyages are integral to many of the Icelandic sagas and their use in the narrative reflects how the Vikings perceived their own world and their understanding of its geography. The Vikings named the places they came to as they explored. As we shall see, this is an important part of transmitting navigational data (see below and pages 28–33 and 36–41).

Navigation was not commonly undertaken away from land, because it was safer to follow a coastline when sailing, but it was done and had been done for a long time before the Viking Age: the Iron Age Hjortspring boat (see pages 18–19) appears to have had similar sailing capacity to a Viking longship. Trials have shown that it could have travelled up to 100 kilometres (60 miles) in one day across the Baltic and that its construction would have enabled it to cope well even in rough seas. It might have been used to visit, raid or trade on any of the Baltic shores.

Traditionally, it was thought that the Vikings used dead reckoning to calculate their position when sailing out of sight of land. The magnetic compass was not invented until the twelfth century and little evidence was available to show how else they might have navigated. It was assumed that they would have been able to estimate their speed based on their knowledge of the ship they were sailing. Direction would have been calculated based on the direction of the sun or stars, and the wind and the sea swell. However, a wooden disc found at Uunartoq in Greenland in 1948 is now thought to have been a compass. It has gnomonic markings on it and the hole in the centre of the disc would have held a wooden rod. This device functioned like a sun dial; rotating the disc until the sun's shadow was aligned with one of the markings on it would have shown in which direction the ship was sailing.

Old Norse literature also mentions a sunstone that helped the Vikings navigate in poor weather. Its existence was doubted until recently, but new research indicates that they would probably have used Iceland spar, a crystal that has polarizing properties. By moving the crystal across the field of vision until a yellow pattern is seen, it is possible to determine, within a few degrees, the direction of the sun in cloudy or foggy conditions, or at twilight (see page 36).

In addition to these two aids, the Vikings made use of landmarks when they were in sight of land. They named many places for their appearance, which would have aided the navigator in determining where the ship was and which direction to sail next. Although Flóki Vilgerðarson is said to have named Iceland for the ice floes in the fjords (see page 36), it is more likely that it was so named because icy glaciers were the first thing to become visible when sailing there on the main route from Norway. Sanday in Orkney and Sandoy in the Faeroe Islands mean "sandy island". A sailor heading to either of these islands would know he had arrived because their names described what he might expect to see upon reaching his destination. Sailing was such an essential part of Viking daily life that many places were named for their appearance from a sailor's perspective. Using these names, it would be possible to describe to someone the route to take to a particular destination with some reliability, despite the fact that the Vikings had no charts from which to work out their course.

With all this in mind, it is clear that the Vikings had relatively sophisticated means of navigating at sea. They could calculate where they were by using the sun, even in poor weather, and their use of descriptive names for the places to which they travelled made it easier to identify if they were in the right place.

ACROSS THE BALTIC AND INTO RUSSIA

While the Norwegians and Danes largely headed west and south, Swedish Vikings headed east across the Baltic and into northern Germany, Poland and the Slavic lands. They both raided and traded there. Excavations have shown that the Baltic was a thriving market before and during the Viking Age, and that trading posts had been established from early on. Towns like Mecklenburg in Germany and Wolin in Poland were similar to the major trading centre at Birka in Sweden and would have fulfilled the same function. Wolin is the town that the Vikings called Jómsborg and was the home of the Jomsvikings, a famous Viking warrior brotherhood. These trading centres were the jumping-off points for Viking exploration into Asia and through to Byzantium and Baghdad.

The journeys of Swedish travellers are commemorated in the legendary *Saga of Yngvarr the Far-Traveller*, which records the exploration of the river systems to the east of Russia. The saga is replete with fantastical detail about the inhabitants along the route, including giants and sorcerers, as well as many encounters with dangerous pagans. Although the Yngvarr of the saga is a legendary character, a Swedish Viking called Ingvarr did travel to the east and there are approximately 26 runestones (see page 86) that commemorate those who travelled with him and failed to return. His voyage is also mentioned in the *Georgian Chronicles*, which are a history of Georgia. Ingvarr's journey took place around 1040 and ended with many of his men being killed while others succumbed to disease, as is reflected in the saga.

From the towns on the eastern side of the Baltic, the Vikings could access the interior of Slavic territories via the Oder and Vistula rivers. From there, they were able to portage, or carry, their ships to the Danube, because the ships were light enough to be dragged around rapids and waterfalls by their crews. Once onto the Danube they could sail all the way to the Black Sea and to Byzantium, although they did have to drag their

OPPOSITE ABOVE These harness mounts from Gotland, Denmark, depict a pair of eagles, a bird that was associated with Odin. Together with wolves and ravens, they were the three beasts of battle that poets described. A great ruler was often said to feed these beasts well, which meant he was successful in battle.

OPPOSITE BELOW A ninth-century bridle-mount found in Lincolnshire. It features decorative faces at both ends and the decorative interlace style indicates that it was produced in Ireland, perhaps in Viking Dublin. Dublin Vikings raided heavily in the Lincolnshire area during the ninth and tenth centuries. This sort of decoration was common on bridles and saddles.

LEFT Runestone in Lindö near Stockholm, Sweden (U 236).
Carved in the eleventh century by the well-known carver
Visäte. The inscription reads: "Ulfr's heirs in Lindey have
raised these stones and made the bridge in memory of
their father and brother. Véseti cut". The monuments thus
comprised multiple stones and a causeway.

ships along some difficult paths to avoid areas of the river that they could not sail through.

Some Vikings travelled east through Finland. Here they encountered plentiful game and fishing, and were able to trade for furs, which were always a valuable commodity. As they travelled further inland, they were able to portage their ships from lake to lake and eventually into the Dniepr and the Volga, and on to the Black Sea. This was important for the settlement of what became Russia, because trading posts were established along their main routes and Scandinavians moved in to settle and trade (see page 86). Staraya Ladoga (*Aldeigjuborg* in Old Norse), which was one of the earliest trading posts like this, has evidence for Scandinavian occupation from the mid-eighth century. At the same time, there is also evidence for occupation by Finno-Ugric, Baltic and Slavic peoples, showing that it was a multicultural melting pot where people met to trade and live together. The importance of trade and the extent of the trading network to which it was attached are emphasized by a hoard of Arabic silver coins that were found there. The coins dated to between AD 746 and AD 786, showing that trade with the Abbasid Caliphate was important even then.

Settlements at Kiev (Old Norse: *Kœnugarðr*) and Novgorod (Old Norse: *Hólmgarðr*) were probably founded in the ninth century as the Scandinavians made inroads into Russia. The *Primary Chronicle*, a Russian history compiled in Kiev in the twelfth century, informs us that the Vikings were making the local tribes pay tribute to them at this time, but were driven back and the tribespeople began fighting among themselves once more. They could not agree peace, so they sought aid from those Vikings who had previously made them pay tribute. Three brothers were chosen to rule over the tribes: Riurik, Sineus and Truvor. Riurik is said to have settled at Novgorod, Sineus at Beloozero in northern Russia and Truvor at Izborsk in western Russia. Shortly after this, Riurik's brothers died and he took sole control of the territory they had been given. The rulers of the Kievan Rus were descended from him (see page 86). This story is legendary only, but it probably indicates the general process of settlement and dominance with occasional setbacks that pertained in this area. It also provides a reason for the naming of the area. The Vikings were known as Rus by the Slavic tribes, so the area was called Russia.

BYZANTIUM AND THE MIDDLE EAST

Once they had reached Russia and the great rivers to the Caspian and Black Seas, the Swedish Vikings sought out Byzantium, the capital of the Eastern Roman Empire, which they called *Miklagarðr*, meaning "big city". Voyages to Byzantium are recorded on 30 Swedish runestones mentioning Byzantium or its inhabitants. These runestones are mainly late Viking Age and commemorate people who died while there. Some were in the Varangian Guard, the personal bodyguard of the Byzantine emperor. Others were merchants who had travelled to Byzantium because it was a major trade centre in its own right.

As the capital of an empire, Byzantium was naturally extremely wealthy and at the nexus of many trade routes. Merchants could buy

OPPOSITE: Skálholt map

In the sixteenth century Sigurd Stefansson from Skálholt marked the sites of the ancient Norse discoveries on a map. His original map has not survived, but a copy made in 1690 by Thordur Thorlaksson is in the Danish Royal Library. Stefansson's positioning of Vinland encouraged archaeological digs at L'Anse Aux Meadows in the 1960s.

Characterum in hac mappa
occurrentium, explicatio
ipsius Auctoris.

A Hi sunt ad quos Angli per
venerunt, ab ariditate nomen
habent, tanquam vel solis vel
frigoris adustione torridi et
exsiccati

B His proxime est Vinlandia
quam propter terræ fœcundi
tatem et utilium rerum ube
rem proventum, BONAM
dixere. Hanc a meridie
oceanum finire voluere no
stri, sed ego ex recentiorum
historiis colligo, aut fretu
aut sinum hanc ab America
distinguere.

C Regionem Gigantum vocant
quod ibi Gigantes cornuti sint
quos Skrickfina dixere.

D Orientaliores sunt, quos klo
fina ab unguibus appella
runt.

E Jotunheimar idem est
ac regio Gigantum mon
strosorum, hic Regiam
Geruthi et Gudmundi fu
isse existimare licet.

F Sinum hic ingentem intelligimus in Russiam excurrentem.
G. Regio petrosa, hujus in historia sæpe fit mentio.
H. Hæc quæ sit insula nescio nisi ea forte quam Venetus ille invenit Frislandiamq Germani vocant.

Autor hujus tabellæ Geographicæ perhibetur esse Sigurdus Stephanius Islandus vir eruditus, Scholæ
Schalholtinæ quondam Rector dignissimus, qui etiam alia nonnulla ingenii et eruditionis specimina edidit
videlicet Descriptionem Islandiæ, quam apud Sereniss. Regiæ Maj. Antiquarium Thormodu Torfæum vidisse me
memini, nec non opusculum de Spletris, quod præterita æstate ab amico quodam in Patria meum
comunicatum, penes me asservatur. Delineationem autem hanc suam, ex antiquitatibus Islandicis
maxima sui parte desumsisse videtur. De Hellulandia Marclandia et Skralingialandia, videri
poterit Arngrimus Ionas, qui ad Calcem opusculi de Gronlandia, Gronlandorum aliquot navigationes
ad has terras annotavit, in terrarum etiam hyperborearum ex ultra Gronlandiam delineatione, ubi
Risaland et Jothunheima collocat, antiquitates quoq Islandicas secutum esse Autorem, sat scio, sed
an authenticæ illæ sint dubito. Cum priore Gronlandiæ mappa Dni Gudbrandi, parum consentire
hanc satis constat. Islandia hic justo majorem habet latitudinem, Promontorium etiam Duriolfsnes, in
gentis continentis potius quam isthmi vel promontorii speciem præfert, ut cætera omittam, quo uni
ca curiositatis potius quam necessitatis ergo hanc mappam annotavi.

goods from all over North Africa, Asia and the Mediterranean. These goods included silk from China, like silk caps found in York and Lincoln. These caps would have been worn, tied under the chin with linen ties, by women. One was recovered at the Coppergate site in York during excavations there; the other was found at Saltergate in Lincoln. Both caps were made from silk that had been cut from the same bale, showing that the goods travelled the great distance to England and were then further traded within England. Other luxury goods also travelled great distances, like spices, fruit and wine that reached Scandinavia from Byzantium.

Before a merchant could trade in Byzantium, he first had to get there. Emperor Constantine Porphyrogenitus wrote that they sailed down the Dniepr and had to negotiate seven rapids, each with names like Gulper, Courser and Yeller. These names have a visual or aural quality that reflects their attributes – they could gulp down ships careless enough to stray into them, or they

ABOVE Sailors dressed as Vikings give a cheery wave from *Hugin*, a replica of the Gokstad ship. *Hugin* was built in 1949 and was sailed to England by a Danish crew, landing at Viking Bay in Kent. She is now on display on the cliffs above Pegwell Bay, Kent.

RIGHT The Oseberg ship in situ during excavation in 1904. The view is from the stern and shows the ornamented keel with the steering oar beside it.

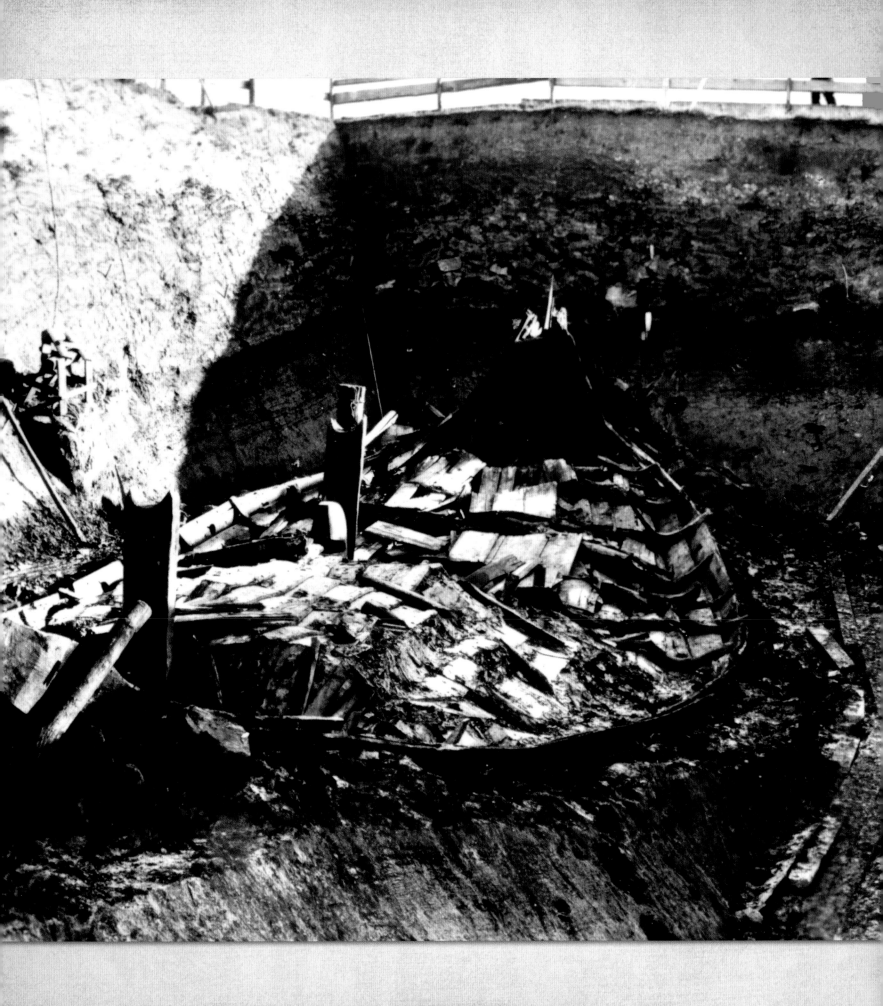

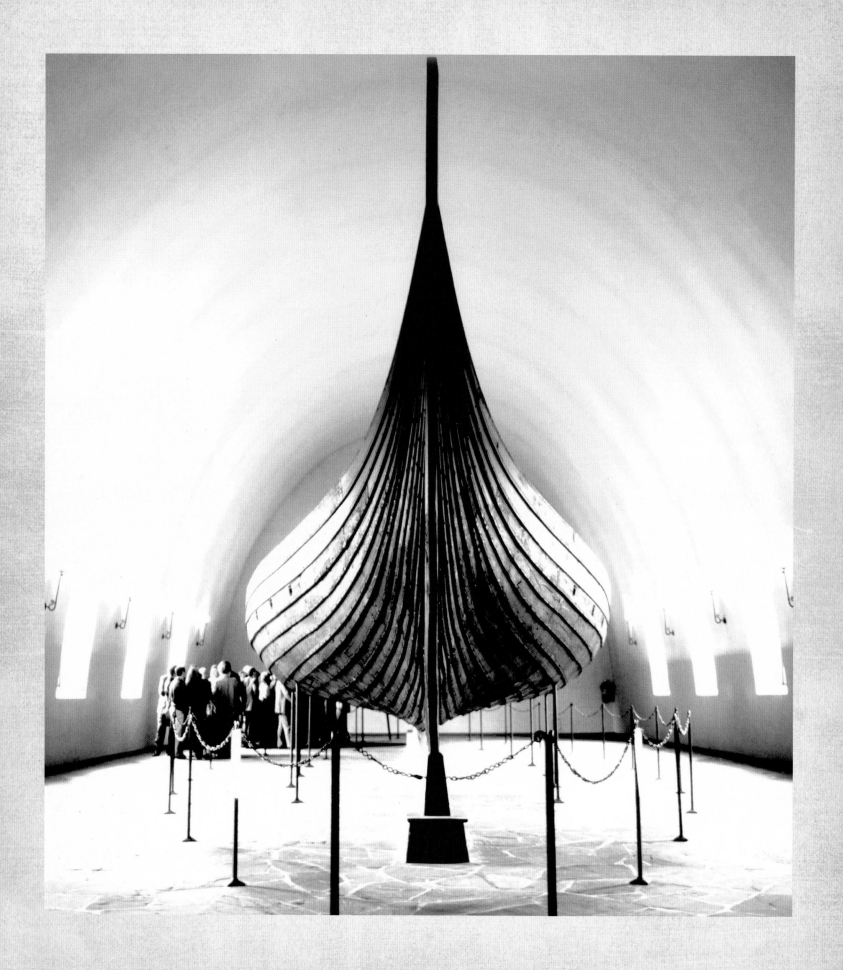

OPPOSITE The Gokstad
Ship was built around
850 AD and used around
900 AD in a burial mound
on the Gokstad farm in
Sandefjord, Norway. The
ship was found in 1880
and is now restored on
display in the Viking Ship
Museum in Oslo.

ABOVE A tenth-century
copper alloy rein-holder
in the Borre style. There
are eight perforated
lugs at the base of the
holder for attaching it
to the harness. It would
have been used to help
prevent the reins of a
draught animal from
getting entangled.

coursed dangerously fast, or made a frighteningly loud noise as the water ran through them. Their names indicate their fearsome nature and the danger they represented. Merchants also had to fend off the assaults of Slavic raiders and then had to cross the Black Sea. It is not surprising that so many runestones were raised as memorials to those who died on this route.

Despite these dangers, the Vikings were not deterred and some even sought to attack Byzantium to take its wealth by force. The first assault by Vikings was made in AD 860 and the last in 1043, with many others between those dates. Other Vikings sought wealth and glory in Byzantium as soldiers of fortune, an even more hazardous profession than being a merchant. Byzantium was often at war and it needed new recruits all the time to replace losses. The Scandinavians' skill at warfare had long been recognized, going back to the days of the Roman Empire, and the Byzantine emperors sought to recruit these doughty warriors. By the end of the eleventh century the emperor's

personal bodyguard consisted almost entirely of Scandinavian mercenaries and they fought throughout the Empire. Harald Hardrada, who fought and lost at the Battle of Stamford Bridge in 1066, was a member of the Varangian Guard in his younger days (see page 58–59). He is said to have become so involved in the politics of the court that he had an affair with the empress, as well as being involved in a coup.

In addition to trading with Byzantium, merchants also traded with the Arab world. The importance of this trade is demonstrated clearly by the vast number of Arab *dirhams* (silver coins) that have been found in Europe. Over 1,000 hoards that include these coins have been found and all are valuable because they make it possible to give an approximate date for the deposition of the hoard, as Arabic coins were marked with the name of the ruler for whom they were minted and with the date of minting.

Contact with the Arab world was not limited to trade. As with the other places they travelled to, the Vikings also raided Arab settlements. Arab historian and traveller Al-Mas'udi wrote that a fleet of Viking ships raided as far afield as Azerbaijan in *c.* AD 913, killing many and taking women and children as slaves. These raiders attacked all around the Caspian Sea and stayed in their base among the islands of the Naptha coast for many months, doing great harm. It was only on their way home again that the Muslim armies were able to attack and defeat the Vikings, who were exhausted by their raiding and burdened by all the loot they had taken. Raids like this are recorded throughout the tenth century and in each the Arab writers emphasize the ferocity of the Vikings, their size and strength and unwillingness to surrender.

Arab writers also give us some of the most detailed descriptions of Vikings. Ahmad Ibn Fadlan travelled north with a Rus party in AD 921. He had been sent on a mission for the Caliph of Baghdad to the king of the Volga Bulgars, and he recorded his impression of the Vikings they met on their travels. He described them as tall, strong, tattooed with dark green designs and never parted from their weapons. Although he stood in awe of their size and strength, he also criticized their cleanliness, claiming that they all shared one bowl of washing water, so that the last to wash received a bowl of filth. Most famously he described the burial rite of a wealthy man, who was laid to rest in a ship that was then burnt. He related how a slave girl was sacrificed with the man and how the person who set fire to the ship had to be naked and walk backwards to the ship with one hand covering his anus while another held a flaming brand for lighting the pyre.

Contact with the Middle East was important from the mid-eighth century, as the coin hoards show. It grew significantly in the mid- to late ninth century, before peaking in the mid-tenth century. After that date it went into rapid decline, because the silver mines of central Asia were exhausted and there was less reason to travel that far.

THE NORTH ATLANTIC AND VINLAND

Where the Swedes headed east and the Danes largely headed south, the Norwegians set out across the North Atlantic. Their primary route was to Scotland and around to Ireland and Wales via the Hebrides. However, occasionally they sailed off course. During these misadventures, they discovered Iceland, Greenland and Vinland (an area of North America), and settled not only these but also Orkney, the Faeroe Islands and Shetland. Thanks to the medieval Icelanders, who were obsessed with writing histories of their country, we have many stories of these expeditions, and the memories of how these places were discovered have been preserved.

Faeroe Islands means "sheep islands", so called because it is said the Vikings found sheep when they first arrived there. The first Norse settlers arrived in the ninth century but recent archaeological evidence confirms that the Faeroe Islands were inhabited before the Vikings arrived there. A Frankish monk, called Dicuil, wrote in *c.* AD 825 that the arrival of the Vikings led to the departure or extermination of the Irish hermits who lived there. If the islands Dicuil was describing were actually the Faeroes, as seems likely, this means that Norse settlers had arrived by that date. *Færeyinga saga*, the *Saga of the Faeroe Islanders*, informs us that Grímr Kamban was the first settler there. His second name is of Irish origin, and it may be that he had spent a lot of time in the British Isles before settling in the Faeroes. However, a runestone was found on the islands dating from the thirteenth century and this records that Torkil Onundarson from

Rogaland in Norway was the first to settle the islands. Whoever it was, they left evidence of their settlement in the form of houses and graves. At the same time as the Faeroes were first being settled, the Orkney Islands and Shetland were also being settled. They had been occupied for thousands of years before the Vikings arrived and were inhabited by the Picts up to the Viking Age. The fate of the Pictish inhabitants remains unknown – they may have been killed, driven out or assimilated into the Viking settlements or they may even have left shortly before the Vikings came.

Like the Faeroes, Iceland may have been occupied by Celtic monks when it was discovered by the Vikings. As with the Picts and the hermits on the Faeroe Islands, their fate is unknown, although in this case *Íslendingabók*, the *Book of the Icelanders*, states that they fled from the Norse settlers. Two people are credited with discovering Iceland by accident in *Landnámabók*, the *Book of Settlements*: Naddoddr, a Norwegian, who was one of the first settlers in the Faeroes, and Garðar Svavarsson, a Swede. Flóki Vilgerðarson was the first person to try to settle in Iceland, but he left after suffering a particularly cold winter. The *Book of Settlements* stated that he named Iceland for the ice floes he saw in the fjords. Ingólfr Arnarson is credited with being the first permanent settler. It is said that he threw the pillars from his high seat overboard into the sea as he approached the land. He then sailed along the coast until he found them and chose that spot to settle. They landed near Reykjavik, and he made his home there in what was to become the capital of Iceland.

The discovery of Greenland is described in *Grœnlendinga saga*, the *Saga of the Greenlanders*, and *Eiriks saga rauða*, the *Saga of Eirik the Red*. Gunnbjörn Ulfsson Kráku is credited with first

ABOVE Calcite Iceland Spar, which may have been used by the Vikings to determine the direction of the sun in poor conditions.

BELOW In the late Viking Age or early Middle Ages, a man called Halfdan carved his name followed by a few more runes on a marble parapet in the Hagia Sophia in Istanbul. Another called Ari or Arni did the same thing on the balustrade in the northern gallery. This Viking Age runic graffiti of Scandinavian names not only illustrates Norse presence in Istanbul, it also shows that several of the Vikings who went there knew how to read and write – at least their own names.

OPPOSITE Seven hoards of treasure, weapons and armour have been found at Gnezdovo in western Russia. Illustrated here is a hoard containing Arab dirhams made into pendants. These date from the second half of the tenth century and are evidence of trade between Kievan Rus and the Islamic world.

The Vinland Map

The Vinland Map was first discovered in 1957, around the same time as the excavations of the Viking settlement at L'Anse aux Meadows. It was presented as a fifteenth-century *mappa mundi* with Vinland, the part of North America discovered by the Vikings marked on it. The map was initially met with suspicion, but it gradually gained credibility. Chemical analysis of the ink and the parchment, however, indicates that the map is most likely a nineteenth-century fake. The debate about this is regularly given new impetus, for instance when new possible sources for the fake are identified.

ABOVE Eiríksstaðir in Haukadalur, Iceland. This is a reconstruction of the Viking Age house on the site where Eirik the Red lived.

having sighted Greenland. He was blown off course while on his way to Iceland from Norway, and sighted land. Eirik the Red set out to find this land after he was outlawed in Iceland for his involvement in some killings. In AD 982 he was banished for three years, which was known in Icelandic law as the "lesser outlawry". Eirik spent the three years of his outlawry exploring Greenland, before returning to Iceland, where he gathered support before setting out to colonize Greenland. The sagas state that he named it Greenland to make it sound more attractive to prospective settlers. Eirik set out with 25 ships but only 14 made landfall in Greenland. Some returned home while others were lost at sea, a fate that was always possible for the Viking sailor. This was the start of the settlement, which was divided into two, the eastern and western settlements, both of which lay close to the southern tip of Greenland.

One ship that set sail with Eirik for Greenland included Herjólfr, the father of Bjarni Herjólfsson. Herjólfr had settled in Iceland but then decided to move to Greenland. Bjarni sailed to Iceland to visit his father in the same year that his father set off for Greenland, so Bjarni decided to follow. On the voyage, Bjarni's ship became lost in fog and he ended up sailing

ABOVE Eiríksstaðir in Haukadalur, Iceland. This is a reconstruction of the Viking Age house on the site where Eirik the Red lived.

ABOVE The reconstructed Norse longhouse at L'Anse aux Meadows, Newfoundland, where Leif Eirikson and Thorfinn Karlsefni attempted to settle c. AD 1000.

off the coast of America. He did not land, but instead, turned around and managed to make his way to Greenland, where he settled. Inspired by the tale that Bjarni told, Leif Eiriksson set sail for this new land. When he arrived there, he sailed down the coast, naming the places they saw. Helluland, meaning "flat stone land", was probably Baffin Island. Markland – "wood land" – was probably the Labrador coastline and finally Vínland, where he settled, was named for the wild grapes that grew there. He stayed the winter, and returned home the following year. Leif's brothers both attempted to settle in Vinland, but Thorvald was killed by natives

and Thorstein died before he could get there. Thorfinn Karlsefni was the next successful settler. He stayed there for two years, during which time the first Viking child was born in Vinland and he fought two battles with the natives, who were called *skraelings* by the Vikings. The last Viking expedition to Vinland was led by Leif's sister, Freydis. It ended in carnage and slaughter, most of which was caused by or carried out by her. After this, no more Viking settlement is known. The excavations at L'Anse aux Meadows in Newfoundland, Canada, have proven that the Vikings did reach America, but not whether it happened as the sagas tell it.

CHAPTER | THREE

RAIDING AND TRADING

ARMS AND ARMOUR

The stereotypical Viking is a large man with a big beard, who is heavily armed (see picture left of vikings at the Battle of Stamford Bridge, 1066). Typical images include a helmet, a coat of mail, a sword, a shield and often a large axe. In fact, the axe may well be the most common weapon with which Vikings are shown. The reality is that, while axes were used, Vikings aspired to owning good swords in the same way as we might aspire to a big house. Bows and spears were common weapons. Most of our knowledge of Viking weapons comes from burials and it can be difficult to differentiate between weapons and tools in some cases. Axes, for example, were used as tools and weapons. Where they were included in burials, they may have been there solely as tools. However, sometimes they are clearly high-status weapons, like the beautifully decorated axe found during the excavation of a grave in Mammen, Denmark (see page 100). Similarly, bows were both hunting and war weapons and it can be difficult to be sure of their purpose.

A good sword cost a lot and so they were the province of the wealthy. Poorer quality swords were certainly available for those who could not afford the best. The Vikings valued most highly old swords; many of these had names like *Grásíða* (grey-flank), *Leggbitr* (leg-biter) or *Naðr* (adder). These swords were valued in part because of their history, but also because an old sword that had survived had proved its superior quality. A warrior would not wish to trust his life to a poor-quality weapon, like the one used by Kjartan in *Laxdæla saga*. Each time he struck with his sword, he had to stand on the blade to straighten it again.

Viking swords typically had distinctive tri-lobed or five-lobed pommels which were most often hollow and attached to an iron upper guard. In some cases swords had solid pommels and no separate guard. In the early part of the Viking Age swords could be single-edged, but the double-edged blade was more common and was almost universal by the end of the Viking Age. Swords were made using a technique called pattern-welding, which involved twisting together bars of iron and forming the sword blade with those. The cutting edge of the sword blade was attached separately and was made from hard steel. This process ensured that the blade was strong and flexible with a good cutting edge.

The Viking spear was designed to be used both as a throwing weapon and as a thrusting weapon. The head could be up to half a metre (1½ feet) long and its shape varied. The head was usually made of iron – sometimes decorated with silver inlay – and could be made using pattern-welding, like a sword blade. The shaft of the spear was made of wood and the spearhead was attached

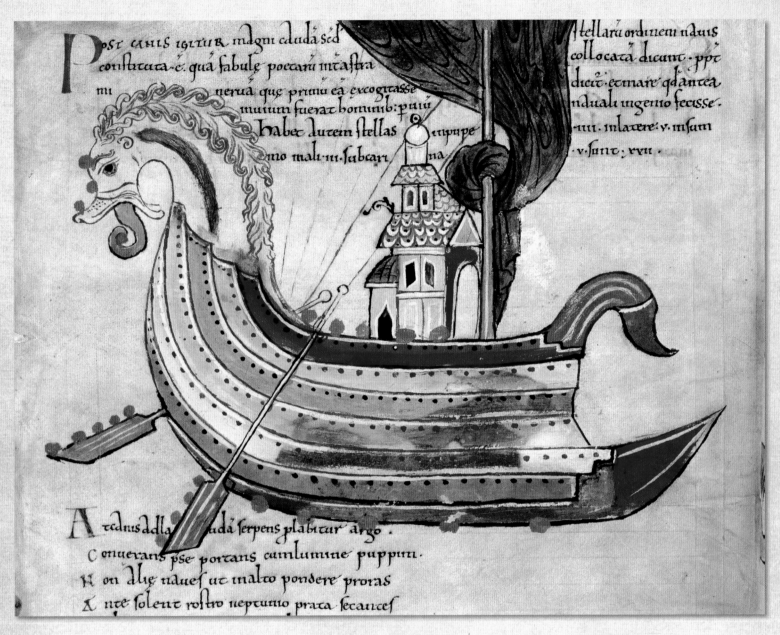

Post canis igitur magni cauda sed
constituta e. qua fabule poetaru intastra
mi   nerua que primu ea excogitasse
muitum fuerat hominib; puu
habet autem stellas   in pupe
mo mali m subcari   na

stellaru ordinem nduis
collocata dicunt. ppt
dicit et mare qd antea
nduali ingenio fecisse.
m. in latere. v. in sum
v sunt; xvii.

A tednis ad la   uda serpens plabitur argo.
C onuerans pse portans cum lumine puppim.
N on alig nduef ut in alto pondere proras
X nte solent rostro neptunio prata secantes

to it with a small rivet. *Grettis saga* tells us that Grettir detached the rivet from his spear in one battle so that, when he threw it, his opponent would not be able to throw it back at him. Other sagas record that certain great warriors were renowned for their ability to throw two spears at once, or to catch a spear thrown at them and throw it straight back to kill the original spear thrower.

Bows were made of wood, such as yew, which is flexible and well suited to this use. A bow made of yew found at Hedeby in Denmark measured 1.92 metres (6 feet 3 inches) long, making it larger than the average English or Welsh longbow, although its draw weight was similar. Arrows were made with iron heads, a wooden shaft with a notch in the end, and the fletching, or feathers, was tied on.

Few examples of Viking Age shields have been found. The ninth-century ship found at Gokstad in Norway included them as part of the burial. They were arrayed along the gunwales of the ship, in the same manner as they would have been carried while the ship was at sea, and were

ABOVE A replica of the Cammin Casket. The original was destroyed during the Second World War. It was a large wooden box decorated with sheets of carved elk horn. The sheets of horn were secured by gilt-bronze bands. It was made in Southern Scandinavia, decorated in the Mammen style and was found at in Cammin, Pomerania. Dating from the early eleventh century, it was probably used as a reliquary.

OPPOSITE The late twelfth-century Baldishol Tapestry depicts personifications of the year. On the left, the young man holding a flower represents April. On the right, the horseman represents May.

painted yellow and black alternately. Old Norse literature records that shields were painted and includes references to shields with stories from mythology depicted upon them, such as the one in the poem *Ragnarsdrápa*. The tenth-century poem *Haraldskvæði* tells us of the *úlfheðnar* (wolfskins) who carried "bloody" shields. This probably means that their shields were painted red, rather than dripping with the blood of their enemies, because other Old Norse sources also refer to red shields. Viking shields were round and made of wood with a central metallic boss, where the warrior held it while in battle. Some may have been faced with leather and some featured metal fittings like those on the shield found at the Sutton Hoo ship burial in Suffolk. The planks of the shield were probably held together by the leather covering and by the wooden fittings behind the shield.

The best armour available to a Viking was mail, made of metal rings joined together. This was expensive and time-consuming to make, so only the wealthy would have owned it. Mail provided protection from the neck to the knees and would have been worn with a leather coat underneath. Those Vikings who could not afford mail would have worn either leather coats or no armour, relying only on their shields for protection.

The typical Viking helmet was a metal cap. The only surviving example of a Viking Age helmet is the one excavated from a farm called Gjermundbu in central Norway, which features a pair of metal "spectacles" attached to the front of the helmet to provide additional protection for the face. This helmet is not decorated, but it is possible that some Vikings had decorated helmets like those found at Vendel and Valsgärde in Sweden, which date to the period immediately

A̅n. dccxci. Herpær baldpulf gehalgod
tobiscop tohpiterne. on xvi. k agustus. fram
eanbalde arcebiscop. 7 fram æþel berhtæ biscop.

A̅n. dccxcii. Her offa myrcna cyning
het æþel bryhtæ þæt heafod of aslean. 7 orred
þepær norð hymbra cyning æfter ppræcsiþe
ham cumenum gelæht pær 7 offlægen. on.
xviii. kł. octob. 7 his lic ligþ æt tunan muðe.
7 æþelred cyning feng to nipan pife seo pær
ælfled gehaten. on. iii. k october.

A̅n. dccxciii. Herpæron reðe fore bec
na cumene ofer norð hymbra land. 7 þæt
folc earm lic bregdon þæt pæron ormete þo
denar 7 ligrescar. 7 fyrenne dracan pæron
gerepene on þam lifte fleogende. þam tacnum
rona fyligde mycel hunger. 7 litel æfter þam
þær ilcan geares. on. vi. id. ianr. earm lice hæ
þenra manna heryunc adilegode godes cyrican
in lindisfarina ee. þurh hreaflac 7 manrliht.
7 sicga forð ferde. on. viii. k martius.

A̅n. dccxciiii. Her adrianus papa. 7
offa cyning forð ferdon. 7 æþelred norðan
hymbra cyning pær offlægen fram hir agenre
þeode. on. xiii. k mai. 7 ceolpulf biscop. 7 eadbald

LEFT: The Anglo-Saxon Chronicle

This page describes the attack on Lindisfarne in AD 793. It relates how terrible portents were seen over Northumberland: great flashes of lightning and dragons were seen in the sky. A great famine (*mycel hunger*) afflicted the people, and then the Vikings descended on God's holy church on Lindisfarne. The manuscript actually states that the attack happened on 8 January, when in reality it took place on 8 June.

ABOVE LEFT A bronze Buddha from the sixth or seventh century AD was found at Birka, Sweden – proof that trading contacts reached into northern India.

ABOVE RIGHT The ninth-century Hon Hoard was found near Hon, Norway in 1834. It included gold coins, brooches and torcs, one of which weighed 1.1 kilogrammes (2 pounds 6 ounces). The coins indicate contact with England, Frankia, Byzantium and the Caliphate.

before the Viking Age. Towards the end of the Viking Age, helmets became conical with a nasal guard providing more facial protection, like those depicted on the Bayeux Tapestry. Many Vikings may have used leather caps, because they could not afford metal helmets.

EARLY VIKING RAIDERS IN EUROPE

Orkneyinga saga tells of Svein Asleifarson, who lived on Orkney in the twelfth century after the end of the Viking Age. Despite being born after the Viking Age, he followed the path of the Viking and his activities may be used to shed light on normal practice for Vikings. He had 80 warriors, whom he kept with him through the winter. He worked his farm in the spring, planting crops and tending to his home affairs. Once he had ensured that the crops

were planted, he would go on a "spring voyage" to plunder the Hebrides and Ireland, returning home just after mid-summer to harvest the crops and ensure that there was enough food for the winter. After that he would go on his "autumn voyage" to undertake more raiding and would return only at the beginning of winter. It is likely that this is how many raiders would have functioned. They had homes and farms that needed to be cared for and, if they failed to get their crops planted and harvested, they would face a hard winter, with little food.

The first recorded attack by Vikings was in AD 789, when three ships arrived at the island of Portland from Scandinavia. The *Anglo-Saxon Chronicle* records that they were crewed by Northmen from Hordaland in Norway. When the local reeve sought to make them report

to the nearby royal town of Dorchester, they killed him (see page 5). Four years later, in AD 793, the famous raid on Lindisfarne occurred and the churchmen of England began to pray to be protected from the fury of the Northmen. Summer raids continued in England throughout the first half of the ninth century, but the pattern changed completely in the second half, when the Viking raiders, whose armies had grown much larger by then, began to overwinter in England and to seek land to settle on.

In the same decade as Lindisfarne was first attacked, Viking raiders descended on the western coast of the Frankish Empire for the first time. As in England, they kept returning every summer for many years but, on the continent, the raiding phase continued much longer than in England. Internal politics in the Frankish Empire, following the death of Charlemagne in AD 814, created disunity, which led to neglect of the coastal defences. Furthermore, the coastal area of Frisia in the north was not readily defensible. The Vikings were sensitive to such opportunities and took full advantage of them. They began to navigate the larger rivers like the Rhine and the

Seine, plundering as they went. Some towns, like the rich Frisian trading town of Dorestad, were raided almost annually for a while. With the death of Louis the Pious in AD 840, matters in the Frankish Empire worsened as civil war ensued, which further played into the hands of the Viking raiders. They even allied with Frankish nobles, as at the raid on Nantes in AD 843, where a rebel Frankish count aided them. To combat Viking raids, the Frankish kingdoms sought to settle Vikings in the coastal areas. These settlers were supposed to prevent new raids but often proved unreliable.

The Irish annals announce that in AD 795 the heathens burnt Rechru and laid waste to Skye. This is the first specific reference to Viking raids in Ireland. The attacks continued thereafter with such a great effect that the monks from the monastery at Iona chose to flee rather than face the wrath of the Norsemen. Those who remained faced new attacks and we are told that 68 of them were slain in AD 806. The monks who wrote the annals recorded numerous examples of Viking atrocities and painted a picture of a reign of terror, but the number of recorded attacks is

ABOVE These coins from the early ninth century were probably minted at Hedeby, Denmark but were found at the trading centre of Birka. Two depict ships while the third shows a beast motif.

OPPOSITE This gilded silver trefoil brooch from the Hon hoard was probably made in Frankia and imported to Norway.

actually quite low for the early period of the Viking raids. In the 820s, the Vikings did indeed step up the number of their raids on Ireland and this continued until, in AD 841, a Viking warband overwintered in Ireland and set up a camp, which was to become the town of Dublin (see page 73). Before that there were no towns in Ireland, but other Viking camps soon followed to provide a base for Viking raids and to act as trading centres for selling the stolen goods.

Although the Viking raids were ferocious and swift, the Vikings did not have things all their own way; there are also many instances of raids that ended in a Viking defeat. Egbert of Wessex defeated a large raid in Cornwall in AD 838 and other raids ended in disaster as happened on Jarrow in AD 794, when some of the raiders' ships were damaged by bad weather and many drowned. Those Vikings who did not drown and made it to shore were slaughtered by the locals. Thus, although they had a fearsome reputation, the Vikings were not always victorious.

PLUNDER AND TRADE

The goal of a Viking raid was to acquire portable wealth easily, which was one reason for targeting churches and monasteries, because these institutions were vulnerable and rich. The possibility of a vigorous defence was generally low and monasteries like Lindisfarne were far enough from the nearest settlement for the raiders to attack and escape before the locals could respond. The fact that they targeted churches and monasteries may be one of the reasons the Vikings gained such a terrible reputation; the monks who wrote the annals that tell us about Vikings would have been inclined to paint those who attacked the Church in the most unfavourable of ways.

Treasure would generally have been anything portable, so gold, silver, livestock and slaves were all viable targets. The Vikings would even prise the decorated mounts from books, like the gilt-bronze mount with eighth-century Anglo-Saxon decoration found in a woman's grave at Bjørke in Norway. Much of our knowledge of Viking treasures comes from hoards that were buried and never collected again, presumably because the people who had buried them did not survive to dig them up or were unable to return to the area.

A hoard found at Stenness in Orkney in 1870 consisted of four gold rings, but most hoards consist solely of silver. The Silverdale hoard, found in Lancashire in 2011, was made up of some 200 items, including silver jewellery and coins. It is thought to have been buried *c.* AD 900. The Cuerdale hoard, also from Lancashire and also dating to the early tenth century, was even larger, with around 8,600 items including silver jewellery, coins, ingots and hacksilver. Hacksilver was pieces of silver cut from other items. The Vikings did not initially have a coin-based currency and would sell goods for a given weight of silver or gold instead. To make up the right weight, they would cut up items and use the pieces as money.

OPPOSITE: Letter from Alcuin to Aethelred of Northumbria

Alcuin of York was a learned cleric in the eighth century. He is known to us from his many writings, among which are a large number of letters. He was living at the court of Charlemagne when the Vikings attacked Lindisfarne in AD 793 and he wrote several letters decrying this act. This one is the letter he wrote to King Aethelred of Northumbria. In it he blames the Viking attack on the decadent nature of Anglo-Saxon society and the way that people indulged their baser desires. He also criticized the desire to follow Scandinavian fashions, especially in the way they cut their hair and trimmed their beards.

annis quod nos nostriq̅ patres huius pulcher
rime patrie incole fuim̅ · & nunquā
talis terror prius apparuit inbrit
tannia · ueluti modo apagana gente
ppessi sumus · nec eiusmodi nauigiū (naufragiū) fieri posse
putabatur; Ecce ecclesia sc̅i cudberhti
sacerdotū dei sanguine aspsa · omnibus
spoliata ornamentis; locus cunctis inbrit
tannia uenerabilior · paganis gentibus
datur addepredandū; Etubi primū
post discessū sc̅i paulini abeuboracia xp̅i
ana religio innr̅a gente sumpsit inciū
ibi miserie etcalamitatis coepit exordiū ·
Quis hoc nontimet? quis hoc quasi captā
patriam nonplangit? uinea electa uulpes
depredarunt · hereditas dn̅i dataest
populo nonsuo; Etubi laus dn̅i · ibiludus
gentiū; festiuitas sc̅auersaest inluctū;
Atenciū considerate fr̅s · & diligentissime
pspicite · neforte hoc inconsuetū m et
inauditū malū aliqua inauditi mali
consuetudine pmereretur; Nondico

Slaves were an important target for Viking raiders. Evidence for slavery takes the form of chains and collars that were used to control the slaves and we find mention of Irish women in the Icelandic sagas. These women may have been taken as slaves to Iceland, because DNA analysis shows that many modern Icelandic women are of Celtic descent. Slaves would not all have been taken back to Scandinavia. Many would have been sold at one of the slave markets in Europe, shipped as far afield as Byzantium, or ransomed back to their family if they were of high enough status.

Although the modern focus is generally on their raiding, trade was already important to the early Vikings. Bristol, though little more than a village at this time, was known as a slave market, as was Rouen in Normandy, and the largest slave markets in Europe were in Spain. The Vikings took slaves from the British Isles and traded them to the rest of Europe, around the Baltic states and to the Byzantine Empire. They also took slaves in eastern Europe and around the Mediterranean to trade in western Europe. For example, Moorish slaves captured in Spain during a ninth-century raid were sold in Ireland. The slave trade flourished during the Viking Age and the Vikings were not the only slavers. English kings captured Vikings and sold them as slaves and most other countries eagerly took part in this trade.

In addition to slaves, the Vikings traded the goods they captured and also those they produced at home. Evidence for this may be seen in silks from Byzantium that were found in Viking York and a bronze Buddha from India that was found in the Swedish town of Birka. Arabic coins from the Caliphate in Baghdad have been regularly found among Viking hoards. Most of these will have passed through many hands to reach the Vikings, but some may have been brought home by Viking travellers. They also traded closer to home. Dorestad – an important trading centre in what is now the Netherlands – was not always raided but was also a trading hub visited by the Vikings. As well as importing exotic goods from further afield, Vikings bought tin, wheat and honey from England, glass, weapons and wine from the Frankish kingdoms, and fur and amber from the eastern Baltic areas. Soapstone was imported from Shetland, while walrus ivory was sourced from Greenland. The Vikings traded with the Sámi peoples in the north of Scandinavia for furs too. Viking merchants had wide-ranging contacts and were connected to a network of other traders that spanned Europe, North Africa and Asia.

LEFT Although most Viking spears would have been made of iron, this one is made of bronze and has a decorated socket. Weapons were often decorated as a mark of status.

OPPOSITE St Edmund was martyred by Viking raiders in the ninth century, when he refused to fight them. This fifteenth-century wall painting from the Church of St Peter and St Paul in Pickering, Yorkshire, depicts the Vikings as medieval English archers.

IBERIA, NORTH AFRICA AND THE MEDITERRANEAN

Spain and settlements on the Mediterranean coast suffered the least from Viking raids, but they did suffer. In AD 843, Frankish sources tell us that the Vikings raided Nantes. There they learnt about the riches of Spain, and so the following year many Vikings headed south with reinforcements from Scandinavia. Their target was the wealth of the Umayyad Caliphate in Spain, or "al-Andalus" as the Arabs called it. The Caliphate had its centre in Damascus, but, at its greatest extent, ruled Spain and North Africa in the west to Afghanistan in the east. As a result, its holdings were rich in treasure, but the Vikings were after more than gold: the biggest slave markets in Europe were in Spain at this time. This raid into Spain was a large one – Arabic chroniclers stated that 54 ships took part. They sailed from their base on the Loire in AD 844 and attempted an attack on the Christian kingdom of Galicia and Asturias, but were driven off, so they headed south to Lisbon, which they sacked successfully. Spurred on by their success, they attacked and plundered Cadiz, Medina Sidonia and Seville in quick succession, then spent some five weeks pillaging the surrounding countryside. The Arabic chronicler Ibn Hayyan described the assaults in detail. He tells us that the Vikings remained in Seville for seven days, killing the men and enslaving the women and children. They then ransomed some of the prisoners back to the Muslims, before setting off again, only to be attacked by a Moorish army that had now been gathered. The Viking raiders were defeated and had to abandon 30 ships because they did not have men enough to crew them. According to Ibn Hayyan, 1,000 Vikings were killed and 400 captured. These survivors were beheaded. As part of this voyage, the town of Asila on the coast of Morocco was also attacked, but little is known of this assault and it appears that only part of the expedition was involved.

Despite this setback, further Viking raids against Spain and the Mediterranean were undertaken. In AD 859 the Swedish king Björn Ironside instigated the only other major expedition into the Mediterranean. His outward journey along the coast of Spain was not particularly successful, but, as soon as his ships entered the Mediterranean, their luck changed. They plundered Algeciras in Spain before raiding al-Mazimma in Morocco. They continued their voyage, pillaging the coasts of Spain and the south of France before overwintering in the Camargue. In the spring of AD 860, they continued to sail eastwards in the Mediterranean as far as Italy, where they sacked the town of Luna. Dudo, the Norman historian, reported that they attacked Luna because they thought it was Rome. After sacking two more towns in Italy, the expedition sailed further eastwards and may have made assaults on settlements in the eastern Mediterranean, but its movements are not clearly recorded.

It is not certain where they spent the winter of AD 860–861, but we do know that in AD 861 Björn and his crews sailed westwards once more. As they travelled past Spain, they were attacked and defeated by a Muslim fleet. The Arab ships in this encounter were equipped with Greek fire – a type of napalm that was launched by catapult, to which wooden ships were especially vulnerable – and they used it to set alight the Viking ships. The survivors sailed on, sacking Pamplona on the way, and capturing the king of Navarre. They ransomed him for 70,000 gold coins before returning home. Of 60 ships that set out, only 20 returned.

After Björn Ironside's expedition, only a small number of further raids were made, presumably because these expeditions had proven so costly to the Vikings. The towns of Spain were well fortified, which made it much more difficult to attack them than the potential profit justified. Moreover, the Caliphate was better organized than the Frankish kingdoms, so it was able to respond to Viking raids better. Although there were few raids, the Vikings still engaged in activities in the Mediterranean. Harald Hardrada (Old Norse *harðráði*, ruthless) was a member of the Varangian Guard in Byzantium from *c.* 1035–

ABOVE A lithograph of the St Brice's Day Massacre, by Alfred Pearse. One of the victims was supposed to have been Gunnhild, sister of Svein Forkbeard, and this was claimed to be one reason why he invaded England in 1013.

1044. As a member, and ostensibly a leader, of this elite body of Scandinavian warriors, he took part in campaigns in and around the Mediterranean. Snorri Sturluson (see page 9) recounts how Harald took the Guard on campaign in the Land of the Saracens (Asia Minor) and conquered many towns there and, in doing so, became very wealthy. Harald is also credited with conquering towns in Sicily by various stratagems. One involved capturing the birds that nested in the thatched roofs of the town and attaching burning wood shavings to them. When the birds flew home to their nests, they set light to the town's roofs and the townsfolk were so dismayed by this that they surrendered. Although Harald's adventures may be exaggerated, they belong to a tradition of stories about him that certainly bolster the image of the man described as the last of the Vikings.

THE GREAT ARMY IN ENGLAND AND ALFRED THE GREAT

In AD 865, the *Anglo-Saxon Chronicle* records that a Danish army overwintered in England for the first time. Known to the Anglo-Saxons as the Great Army, this was led by Ivar the Boneless, Halfdan and Ubbi, the sons of the legendary Norse king Ragnar Lothbrok, and marked the beginning of the conquest of the area of northern and eastern England known as the Danelaw (see page 62).

At this time, England was divided into the kingdoms of East Anglia, Mercia, Northumbria and Wessex. The *Anglo-Saxon Chronicle* states that the East Anglians were able to buy peace by giving the Vikings horses, which they rode northwards the following year to attack York. There was an internal dispute in Northumbria in AD 866, because the Northumbrians had deposed King Osberht, and taken as king Ælla, who was apparently not of the royal line. This discord meant that the Northumbrians were slow to respond to the

Viking attack on York. When they did, they were able to break into the town, but then the Vikings slaughtered them and killed both their kings in the battle. The survivors had to make peace.

In AD 867, the Vikings rode to Nottingham, which was in Mercia. There they occupied the fortification and the combined might of Mercia and Wessex could not shift them, so the English had to broker a peace treaty. The Great Army returned to York the following year and then in AD 869 rode once more to East Anglia, where they took up quarters at Thetford and fought a battle with Edmund, the king of East Anglia. They defeated and captured Edmund, and are said to have amused themselves after the battle by shooting arrows at him and then beheading him, because he would not renounce his Christianity. For this death, Edmund was declared a saint and martyr.

Following this, the Great Army continued to wreak havoc across the English countryside until, in AD 871, they attacked Wessex, supported by another army that had arrived under Guthrum. They were beaten by an army under Ealdorman Aethelwulf at Englefield near Reading, but continued their invasion. King Aethelred and his brother Alfred attacked the Great Army near Reading and were beaten, but rallied their army and met the Vikings four days later at Ashdown, where they defeated the Great Army. Asser – a Welsh monk who became Bishop of Sherborne and later was a member of Alfred's court – wrote a life of Alfred in which he declares that Alfred had to begin the battle without Aethelred and his men, because Aethelred refused to fight until he had finished hearing mass. Shortly after Easter of AD 871, Aethelred died and Alfred succeeded to the kingdom. The Great Army fought several more battles against the West Saxons that year and won more often than not, so the Saxons sued for peace and presumably had to pay the Great Army to stay away. This peace treaty ensured that Wessex was left in peace for five years.

In subsequent years, the Mercians were afflicted by the Great Army. They too bought their peace at great price two years in succession, but their bribery did not work and the kingdom collapsed when the Great Army occupied the royal centre at Repton in Derbyshire. A mass grave excavated in the vicarage garden at Repton during the 1980s contained approximately 250 skeletons, the majority those of men in the prime of life, while a small number were women. The dating evidence suggests that this mass grave was for members of the Great Army who had succumbed to disease while the army was overwintering there.

With Mercia and Northumbria in Viking hands, it was only to be expected that Wessex would follow. Half the Great Army chose to settle on the lands they had conquered, but the other half chose to attack Wessex. This army was led by Guthrum. It marched through Wessex and seized Wareham in Dorset. Alfred in turn besieged the army but could not force it to surrender. In the end a treaty was agreed and the Vikings swore on a sacred arm ring to uphold the peace. Alfred, a Christian king, had sought to use the Vikings' own pagan ritual of swearing oaths on a sacred ring to bind them to the treaty. The two armies also exchanged hostages as a token of their commitment to the treaty. However, Guthrum and his troops slipped away at the first opportunity after killing all the hostages they held. Alfred was only able to enforce peace when reinforcements for the Viking army were wrecked as they tried to sail to meet it.

The peace did not last long. Guthrum returned in AD 878 and caught Alfred by surprise. Alfred was forced to flee into the marshes of Athelney, from where he might try to rebuild his army. When he was ready, Alfred sought out the Vikings and fought a great battle at Edington, where he defeated them in the field and besieged those who retreated into their fort until they surrendered. Guthrum agreed to be baptized, taking the name Aethelstan as part of that baptism, and Alfred accepted him as his adoptive son. With this victory and the resultant treaty Alfred secured his kingdom. The Vikings who did not wish to settle sought easier plunder in France, which resulted eventually in the break-up of the Carolingian Empire in AD 888. Alfred still had to contend with Viking raids, but not on the scale that had previously assailed him.

At home, King Alfred set about reforming his kingdom. He introduced military reforms that would enable his son Edward the Elder and his grandson Aethelstan to conquer England. The reforms included establishing a network of forts (*burhs* in Old English) to protect Wessex. Alfred began building a fleet to defend his realm at sea and he introduced educational reforms to ensure that as many people as possible could read. Alfred also began translating books into his own language. At some point shortly

OPPOSITE *King Canute Defies the Waves* by James Edwin McConnell. To convince his courtiers that he was not all-powerful, Canute set his seat on the beach and command the waves to retreat, knowing that they would not.

after conquering London in AD 886, Alfred also drew up a treaty with Guthrum that defined the Danelaw, the kingdom where Danish law prevailed. The boundary between the two kingdoms was to be along the Thames to the Lea, from the Lea to Bedford and then up the Ouse to Watling Street. South of this line was Wessex, north was the Danelaw.

DANEGELD: THE DANISH RESURGENCE AND THE RISE OF CNUT THE GREAT

The Icelandic manuscript *Fagrskinna* (meaning "fair parchment") records that Olaf Tryggvason, who was to become king of Norway in AD 995, set out with a fleet on a raiding voyage in the late tenth century. He circumnavigated the British Isles, raiding as he went, before travelling to France to raid there. The *Anglo-Saxon Chronicle* records that Olaf Tryggvason led the Viking band that landed at Maldon in AD 991 and fought Ealdorman Byrhtnoth. This battle is commemorated in the Old English poem *The Battle of Maldon*, which is thought to have been written shortly after the battle. The poem describes how the Vikings defeated Byrhtnoth and names those Anglo-Saxons who ran from the battle first as well as the heroes who stood and died beside their leader. To make the Vikings go away, King Aethelred, who is known to us as "the Unready", paid them 4,500 kilograms (10,000 pounds) of silver. According to the *Anglo-Saxon Chronicle*, this was the first time that Danegeld – a tax to save a land from ravage (see page 63) – was paid, but it was not

to be the last. Olaf's voyage was not the first in the resurgence of raiding, but it is certainly one of the best documented, not least because it culminated in his baptism and conversion to Christianity. This raiding voyage was part of a new era of raiding that was to cause significant political problems for England.

The second series of Viking raids on Britain was probably partially a result of increasing centralization of power in Scandinavia and partially a result of the exhausting of silver reserves in the Middle East. Arabic silver had been a mainstay of the Scandinavian economy but, as it ran out, so did the eastern trade routes and new sources of wealth had to be found. Combined with the weakness of the English crown, conditions were perfect for a renewed assault following 26 years of relative peace. Raids started to occur once more in the AD 980s and increased in size to the extent that Olaf's raid in AD 991 was said to consist of 93 ships. Paying Olaf off did not prevent others from raiding England, and Olaf himself returned just three years later in company of Svein Forkbeard, King of Denmark. They had 94 ships and attacked London itself. They were driven off from London, but continued to harry the countryside until King Aethelred offered them 7,250 kilograms (16,000 pounds) of silver and the provisions they needed in return for leaving.

Olaf never returned to attack England, but others, including Svein, were continued to raid and extort Danegeld from the English. The raids reached such a peak that King

Aethelred, fearing a conspiracy to oust him from his throne, ordered that all the Danish men in England be slaughtered on St Brice's Day (13 November) in 1002. Evidence for the extent of this massacre is sparse: a charter to St Frideswide's Abbey in Oxford refers to Danes being slaughtered and the bodies of 34–38 young men, who died around this time, were found at St John's College, Oxford, in 2008. Other evidence for wholesale massacre of Danes is not present, which suggests the massacre was more localized. It also seems unlikely that Aethelred's orders would have been carried out at all within the Danelaw areas. Legend tells us that Svein Forkbeard's sister was one of the victims and that his later invasion of England was partly motivated by this.

If the massacre did occur, it did not deter the Vikings from continuing their depredations. Raids continued for another ten years and the Danegeld paid in 1012 was as much as 21,700 kilograms (48,000 pounds) of silver. England was in a poor state by this time, although its tax collection system had been refined and made more efficient as a result of the Viking raids.

In 1013 Svein Forkbeard returned to England as an invader, not as a raider. Much of England submitted to him very quickly, but the south held out longer until Aethelred fled to Normandy at Christmas time. Svein was now the ruler of England and Denmark, but was to enjoy his reign for only five weeks before he died. Aethelred returned to rule England and did so until Cnut, Svein's son, invaded in 1015. Cnut

seized Northumbria and prepared a campaign to take the rest of England. Aethelred died in April 1016 and his son, Edmund Ironside, succeeded to the throne. Edmund fought a largely successful campaign against Cnut all through that year until he was betrayed to Cnut by his own people at the battle of Ashingdon. Shortly after that, he and Cnut agreed a treaty that divided the country between them. Edmund retained Wessex, while Cnut got the rest of the country. Edmund lived only until November 1016, after which Cnut gained the whole of England and ruled it until his death in 1035. He was a strong and effective king who introduced some Danish customs to England, but England also influenced Denmark. For example, Cnut appointed several Englishmen as bishops in Denmark, and even today most of the ordinary Danish words of church organization are English in origin. At the height of his power, Cnut ruled an empire that consisted of Denmark, England, Norway, Orkney and south western Sweden.

Cnut appointed his son Harthacnut as his heir, but his other son Harald was chosen by the English as king. Cnut's Norwegian holdings were lost to Magnus the Good, whom the Norwegians took as king. Harthacnut took the throne in England only when his brother died in 1039, and he was succeeded by Edward the Confessor in 1042. With that, Danish rule in England ended, but the Viking Age would not end until 1066, when Harald Hardrada, king of Norway and the last of the Vikings, fell in battle at Stamford Bridge (see page 119).

OVERLEAF Close-up of the Cuerdale hoard. Found in 1840 in Lancashire, this is still one of the largest Viking silver hoards found to date. The hoard is dated to the early tenth century and contains c. 8,600 items including silver jewellery, coins, ingots and hacksilver (see page 52).

CHAPTER FOUR

SETTLEMENT ABROAD

The Norse did not go abroad only to raid or trade as Vikings, they also settled and founded Norse colonies in various parts of the Viking world. Some of the areas they settled were relatively uninhabited, like Iceland, while others required a lot of contact with the existing population, resulting in a certain amount of assimilation, such as in England.

THE NORTH ATLANTIC: THE FAEROE ISLANDS, ICELAND AND GREENLAND

In the early to mid-ninth century, the Vikings reached the Faeroe Islands in the Atlantic (see page 34). The islands had much to offer: good pastures, enough land to grow crops, and a large population of seabirds on the cliffs. The Vikings had to import wood, but the sea would also have supplied driftwood. Most of the archaeological finds of household and luxury items were imported from Norway, Shetland or England. The Viking settlers were very well connected to the rest of the Viking world. In the early phase of the settling, farmsteads and outhouses were built further up the hills for seasonal use, and in the eleventh century the descendants of the Norse settlers built a wooden church.

The Vikings discovered Iceland in the mid- to late-ninth century. They found a practically uninhabited land (see page 36), with good pastures and fishing grounds. There also were, like today, natural hot-water basins and spectacular geysers. Less attractive, though equally fascinating, must have been the reeking sulphur pools and the rough, yet eerie, lava fields. The glaciers that covered most of the island were of course familiar to Norwegian Vikings and, contrary to popular belief, the Vikings did find trees there. The forests were, however, much less sustainable than in Norway and, as trees were felled to serve as timber for houses and fuel, the soil eroded so that the wooded areas could not recover from deforestation. The land was quickly surveyed and the settlers claimed fjords, valleys and headlands for themselves.

Two important books were written about this period in the twelfth century. *Íslendingabók* (*The Book of the Icelanders*) and *Landnámabók* (*The Book of Settlements)* mention who the first settlers were and how they divided the land. There was no substantial native population the Vikings had to interact with, but they still made some changes to their customs and culture, most notably in how they organized themselves politically in the new country. It seems the first settlers claimed large pieces of the best land. Subsequent newcomers were then allocated parts of these lands. Despite this hierarchy, the Icelanders felt equal to each other – there is no evidence of people who established themselves as significantly more rich and powerful than the others. This egalitarian society also resulted in the establishment of the *Althing*, the yearly general assembly which every free man had to attend. The assembly was held at Thingvellir, a sheltered, yet accessible place with natural acoustics and plenty of camping space. It was at the *Althing* that law was spoken and it was also where the Icelanders officially accepted Christianity in the year 1000 (see page 114). The Icelanders kept in close contact with their homelands, not only to trade and import the necessary goods, but there was also a flourishing tradition of Icelandic poets trying their luck at the courts of Norwegian kings.

Greenland was first settled by Eirik the Red (see picture of Brattahlid in Greenland on page 66), who was convicted of murder and banished from Iceland for three years (see page 40). The existence and rough location of Greenland were known, but Eirik was the first to explore the island to see if it was worth settling, and after his banishment he returned to Iceland to recruit a party of settlers. The settlers are said to have found traces of the indigenous population, but there seems to have been limited contact between the two, occurring only when the Norse went further north on long-distance hunting expeditions. Eventually, there were two extended settlements on Greenland, which became Christian even before Iceland – and the colony flourished for several centuries until conditions changed.

From Greenland, Vikings regularly travelled to the coast of North America (see page 34). They established a small settlement at L'Anse aux Meadows, which was short-lived, however. It seems it was not maintainable because of the long distance to Greenland and too many hostile encounters with the native populations.

LEFT A view from the altar end of the church at Birsay. The Brough of Birsay was inhabited by Picts, who left a picture stone there, until Norse settlers displaced them. The church is Norse and the remains of Norse houses are visible on the Brough. Excavations have shown remains of a Pictish graveyard beneath the Norse church.

OPPOSITE ABOVE The Ring of Brodgar at Stenness, Orkney, would have been a landmark for Orkney Vikings. This Neolithic henge would have been known to the Orkney pilgrims mentioned in *Orkneyinga saga*. One of the standing stones is carved with a runic inscription in twig-runes similar to those in Maeshowe, but it is uncertain if this is a genuine inscription from the Viking Age or early Middle Ages.

OPPOSITE BELOW Birsay Bay, Orkney. The Brough of Birsay on Birsay Bay was home to Pictish, Norse and later settlements between the seventh and thirteenth centuries.

BELOW Remains of the Norse church near Hvalsey (modern-day Qaqortoq), Greenland. This church was built in the fourteenth century in the area where the Norse settled and is exceptionally well-preserved. There presumably was an earlier church here too.

SCOTLAND, ORKNEY, SHETLAND AND THE HEBRIDES

There are no written sources that date the first Norse settlement in Scotland or that document the nature of the settlement process. The archaeological material, however, shows that a permanent Norse presence emerged in parts of Scotland from the mid-ninth century onwards. The settlers came mostly from Norway, and the Northern Isles are only two days' sailing distance from there. The landscape of the islands and the Scottish west coast, though much less mountainous, resembles the Norwegian coastal region in the way the sea influences the weather and in the presence of small islands from which sea routes and access to land could be controlled.

It is often assumed that the Vikings first established bases on Scottish territory to serve as stopovers or starting points for attacks on more southern parts of the British Isles. At this time, Scotland was inhabited by Celtic peoples – being, roughly, from north to south the Picts, the Scots and the Britons – of whom many were Christian. Norse leaders seems to have replaced the leading Celtic classes relatively quickly and it is uncertain what happened to these peoples under Viking rule.

It is clear that the Vikings quickly established a successful colony and prospered from effectively controlling the seascape around Scotland and the Irish Sea. Norse settlers exploited the natural resources and they also introduced (not always on purpose) some animals, like particular types of field mice, and plants, such as flax, from Scandinavia to the natural environments, though on a smaller scale than in Iceland. There are remains of several settlements, such as Jarlshof on Shetland, high-status burials, such as at Scar, Sanday, Orkney, and a few rich silver hoards, among them the one from Skaill on the Scottish mainland. Norse farmsteads and cemeteries were often located at pre-existing sites, such as on the Brough of Birsay, Orkney, where there had been a Pictish settlement. In the Northern Isles, there are many more place-names of Scandinavian, rather than Pictish, origin. This shows that there was much less interaction with the people who lived there than in the West Highlands and Isles, where the place-names show a far greater mix of the Norse and Gaelic languages. It is also rather telling that Norse settlers in the Western Isles were quite happy to give their children Gaelic names (which also suggests marriages between Vikings and Celts), while Pictish personal names

BELOW These gaming pieces were found on the Isle of Lewis in 1831. They were made in Norway from walrus ivory in the third quarter of the twelfth century, most likely for export to the Norse rulers of the Scottish Isles. The collection comprises pieces from up to four gaming sets for both Chess and the Viking game of tafl.

were not taken into use by the Scandinavians who settled in the Northern Isles.

This period features in several historical and literary sources from the twelfth century and later, such as Irish and Frankish monastic annals, *Orkneyinga saga*, the life of St Magnus, and *Eyrbyggja saga*. Some of the sources are very succinct, others contradict each other and they are all rather far removed from the events, in time or in place or both. The Scandinavians did leave runic inscriptions by their own hand, mostly on Orkney, but also some on Shetland and mainland Scotland. These inscriptions are also not from the time of the settlement, but date to the later Viking Age. And, although *Orkneyinga saga* describes travellers taking refuge from harsh winter storms in the Neolithic burial chamber Maeshowe (Orkahaugr in the saga) and mentions that two men went mad while sheltering there, we cannot be certain whether the twelfth-century carvers of the approximately 33 Old Norse runic inscriptions in the chamber were travelling Scandinavians, or people whose families had settled in Orkney generations ago. There are a small number of cross slabs and commemorative stone crosses with Old Norse runic inscriptions that illustrate how the Scandinavian tradition of raising runestones as memorials for the dead and the native tradition of Christian stone sculpture were combined.

IRELAND AND THE ISLE OF MAN

The Viking settlement in Ireland had a different character. Where the settlement in Scotland was mostly of a rural character and the nature of the contact with the Celtic inhabitants is unclear, in Ireland the Vikings founded urban trading centres, most importantly Dublin, and they traded extensively with the Irish and England. They also met with fierce resistance from the Irish kings when they tried to expand beyond Dublin.

Dublin was first used in the ninth century by the Vikings as one of their several longphorts in Ireland, camps where they could gather for further raids. After this phase, when Dublin became a place of permanent settlement, the Scandinavians undertook a reorganization of the settlement. Houses were built on fenced plots all facing the streets. There were defensive ramparts around the town, on the other side of which were further living quarters and the hinterland that supplied the town with food and resources. It is unknown to what extent this land was also in Scandinavian hands, but if not, there was certainly a lot of what seems to be peaceful interaction with the surrounding population. The Norse settlers used Dublin's strategic situation on the Irish Sea to its full advantage and the town became a very wealthy trading centre, so raiding became less and less important. The silver hoards that were buried in the area show that the Dublin Norse began to adopt an economy with payments in coins rather than in bullion or hacksilver relatively early, compared to the Scandinavian homelands. This was probably a result of their extensive contact with the English economy.

The Isle of Man also knew a strong Norse presence. The Viking settlers came from Norway, Denmark, Scotland and Ireland, but the island was most closely tied to the Northern Isles. The Earls of Orkney held power over the Isle of Man and later the Manx kings ruled the Hebrides. At a later stage the trade contacts with the Western Isles, Dublin and Chester became more important and the silver hoards of the wealthy Isle of Man again show an early preference for coins over bullion. On Man, as in Ireland and England, there was much more interaction with the Manx population of Christians. This resulted,

for instance, in a hybrid type of commemorative stone monument. The Viking settlers became Christians in the course of the tenth century and then adapted the Manx tradition of memorial stones. They added their art styles and motifs, which were also used on the runestones and picture stones of Scandinavia, such as Sigurd the Dragonslayer. Runic inscriptions in Old Norse are carved on several of these monuments.

ENGLAND AND THE DANELAW

After the first phases of raiding, the Vikings established bases where they could overwinter and undertake further raids, such as at Repton. This meant that from the mid-ninth century the Vikings became a permanent presence in England. From AD 866 onwards, the Vikings went to England in greater numbers than before (called the Great Army by the Anglo-Saxons, see page 59). They became more focused on taking land and settling there. In a time of internal power struggles among the people of East Anglia, Northumbria and Wessex, the Vikings were able to win large parts of the country relatively quickly. Just over a decade later, the Vikings controlled Northumbria, East Anglia and Mercia. The lands previously held by the Anglo-Saxon aristocracy and the Church were now distributed by the war leaders among "their" Vikings, and the *Anglo-Saxon Chronicle* notes that "they proceeded to plough and support themselves". All the while the Vikings were also trying to conquer Wessex, when finally they lost battle in AD 878 against King Alfred (see page 60). A truce was settled between the Anglo-Saxons and the Scandinavians and a treaty was drawn up, resulting in the establishing of what

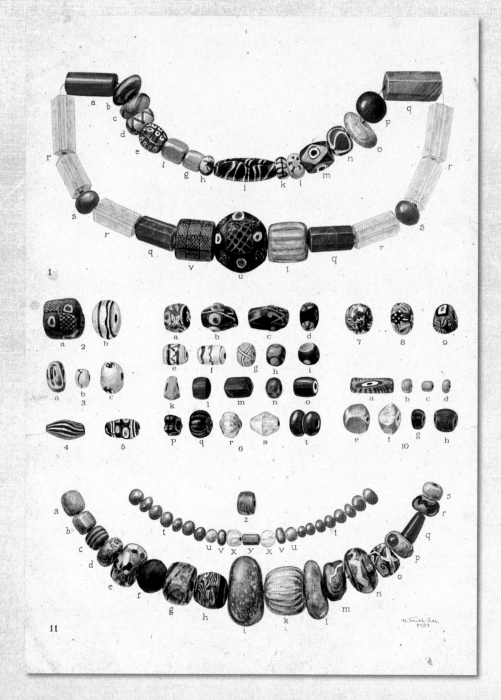

Drawing of glass beads found in tenth-century graves in Birka, Sweden

This drawing was made as part of the excavation report. The drawing shows the colourful variety of beautiful bright glass beads that were worn by Viking women.

OPPOSITE Oval brooches by chains of beads were typical pieces of women's jewellery. They were always ornate and a chain would hang from them with the keys to the house on it. In the Viking Age, women had charge of the keys. These brooches were found in Sweden.

OVERLEAF A Viking Age cord road is visible in the foreground of this excavation in Dublin, Ireland. Even after being defeated at the Battle of Clontarf in 1014, the Vikings continued to live in Ireland.

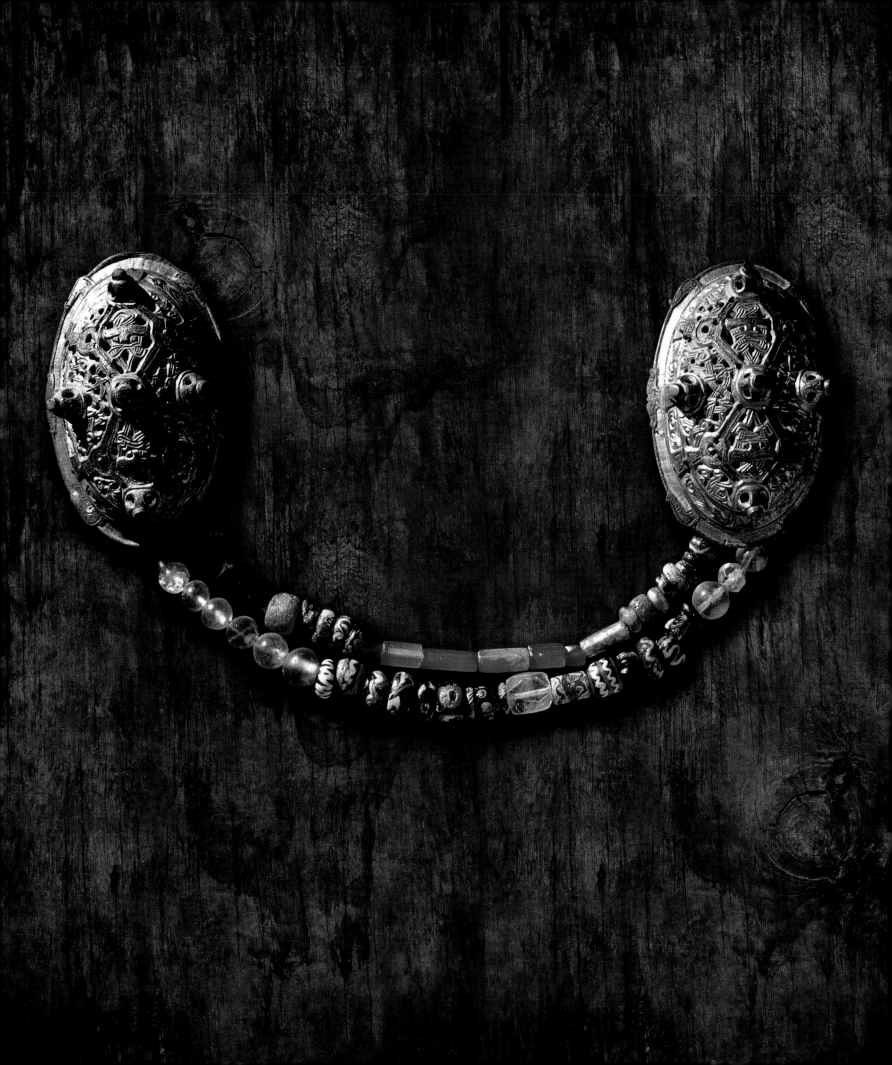

became known as the Danelaw (see page 62). King Alfred held Wessex and part of Mercia, while Northumbria, East Anglia and the rest of Mercia were officially under Scandinavian control. This truce was fragile, however, and the Vikings based armies at strategic places to consolidate their power. Such places were not only politically significant, they were also centres of economic importance. These towns, such as Derby, Leicester, Lincoln, Nottingham and Stamford, naturally became important in the English campaign for recovering the country.

The Vikings quickly recognized the importance of coins in claiming and maintaining leadership over an area. They employed minters from the continent to imitate the coins that King Alfred issued. The Viking coins were, like the Anglo-Saxon tradition, struck in name of patron saints, but some designs also incorporate images of a sword and a Thor's hammer.

Despite the violent colonization process, the Vikings integrated quickly in their new Anglo-Saxon homelands. They converted to Christianity and soon adopted the customs and conventions. This quick integration, however, does not mean the Scandinavian culture was totally dissolved. On the contrary, there are many indications that a new Anglo-Scandinavian culture emerged.

RIGHT This stone cross at St Mary's church, Gosforth, was carved in the tenth century. The area saw an influx of Viking settlers arriving in the ninth and tenth centuries. Norse influence on Anglo-Saxon stone sculpture is visible in the decoration, which includes scenes from Norse mythology as well as the crucifixion of Christ.

0   1   2   3
inches.

**Viking ship incised in stone,
from Jarlshof, Shetland**

There was a Norse settlement at this pre-existing Pictish location from the ninth century onwards, with a longhouse, and several other houses and outbuildings. Several stone slabs with incised drawings were found here, including this one of a dragon's head at the prow of a Viking ship.

The most striking result of this is demonstrated by stone sculptures, which shows remarkable innovation. Anglo-Saxon stone monuments were produced in a monastic context for the upper ranks of the Church and the aristocracy. By contrast, the Scandinavian memorial stone tradition was much more secular and included a wider section of society. The Viking influence took the stone sculpture out of the monastic context.

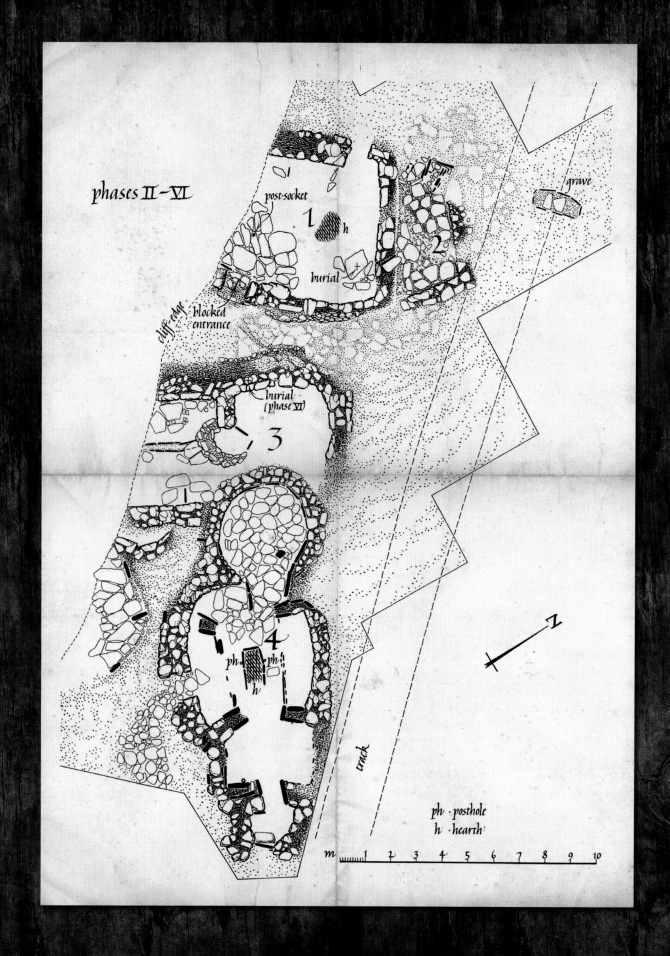

phases II – VI

post·socket

grave

1   h
burial

blocked
entrance

cliff·edge

burial
(phase VI)

3

4
ph   ph
h

track

ph · posthole
h · hearth

N

m ⅢⅢⅢⅢⅢ 1   2   3   4   5   6   7   8   9   10

Excavation plan of Buckquoy settlement , Mainland Orkney

The settlement at Buckquoy, facing the Brough of Birsay, was excavated in 1970–71. Remains from the Norse phase of the settlement include a mid- to late-tenth-century grave dug into the mound that was formed by the ruins of three successive Norse long-houses. The man was buried with, among other things, a bronze ring-pin and half of a silver penny of Edmund (ad 940–6), while the finds from the houses include bone combs, flat spindle whorls and a stone game-board.

Memorial stones and grave monuments were now carved by secular professionals who also served a wider, though still elite, clientele. Scandinavian art styles and motifs were introduced and new shapes and forms of monument were developed. The most conspicuous of these new monument types are gravemarkers called hogbacks. They seem to originate in Yorkshire, and they are mostly found in that region, but there also are a few in Derbyshire, Scotland and Ireland.

York was a significant town for the Viking settlers. It was important for controlling north-west England and was already an established trading centre. The town was developed

ABOVE An eleventh-century fresco in the Cathedral of Saint Sophia in Kiev. It depicts a fight between two warriors, one masked and stripped to the waist. The fresco probably records the visit of the Princess Olga to Byzantium in AD 953, when Viking Rus warriors performed a sword dance as entertainment. The masked man may be one of the only depictions we have of a Viking berserker.

ABOVE Thingvellir in Iceland. Öxará (Axe River) runs through the middle of Thingvellir, where the Icelandic annual national assembly (*Althing*) was held. The area is now a national park, where the remains of the assembly-goers' booths are still visible.

further under Viking reign as a well-organized production centre and its place in the Viking Age trading network grew. It remained in Viking hands even after the English had taken the Five Boroughs – these were the five main towns of Mercia: Derby, Leicester, Lincoln, Nottingham and Stamford – and by AD 920 it was all the Danish Vikings had left since they had lost more and more of their territory to the English under the reign of King Edward and his sister

Aethelflaed. In subsequent decades, while the rest of England was mostly under English rule, York repeatedly changed hands between Dublin Vikings and the English, until Eric Bloodaxe was defeated at Stainmore in AD 954. Although the whole of England was now united under one English king, the descendants of the Great Army remained an important part of the population, and close to a century of Viking rule left marks in the language, landscape and culture.

DUKE ROLLO AND NORMANDY

In the early tenth century, the Viking presence on the river Seine was becoming so disruptive that the Frankish ruler made the strategic decision to grant land to the leader of one of the bands of Vikings if they would settle there and defend Frankia against attacks by other Viking troops. Hrólfr, or Rollo in French, and his men settled accordingly on their land in the east of what is now called Normandy. Subsequently, Rollo and, after him, his son William Longsword and their Vikings expanded their territory via political negotiation and raiding and defined modern Normandy.

Rouen was an important administrative centre, where William Longsword established his mint, and a flourishing trading centre that was well connected to the international trading networks. The place-name evidence from Normandy suggests that some of the settlers were Vikings from Scandinavia, particularly Denmark, and some were Vikings from Ireland. The archaeological material shows that, as in England, the settlers were quick to convert to Christianity, which undoubtedly helped with the rapid assimilation between the Scandinavians and the Frankish population. This part of the Frankish Empire remained under Viking rule, which soon merged into Norman rule, and the duchy of Normandy grew strong enough to conquer England in 1066.

THE KIEVAN RUS

In the late ninth century the Rus state had expanded southwards from the Novgorod region to include Kiev as its capital. The population of the Rus state was predominantly Slavic, but the rulers had Norse names. In the early- and mid-tenth century the Kievan Rus tried to expand further into Byzantium by attacking Constantinople, but they had to settle for treaties which gave them trading privileges. In AD 988 the Kievan ruler converted to Greek Orthodox Christianity and married the Byzantine emperor's sister, which improved the Rus' relations with Byzantium even more, and by this time the Rus already had a much more Slavic than Scandinavian identity. This even happened in the settlements of Staraja Ladoga, Gorodice and the town of Novgorod, which were situated much closer to Scandinavia. The latter town especially knew a sophisticated, rich artisan and merchant milieu with a well organized political system. The Scandinavian early Rus mostly focused on expanding their territory and the lucrative long-distance trade, but Viking warriors also enrolled in the armies of the Byzantine Emperor. When the emperor formed a new personal guard in the late tenth century, many of the elite fighters were Scandinavians, the Varangian Guard (see page 33). There were also Vikings in this Varangian Guard who came directly from Scandinavia, and they had a much stronger Norse identity than the Rus at this point. Being in the Varangian Guard was a high-status job, which came with many privileges and good payment. Several runestones in Scandinavia commemorate men who travelled to – and often died in – the east, and it is thought that some of these men served in the Varangian Guard or may have travelled there on trading or raiding expeditions (see page 28).

RIGHT Öxará Waterfall near Thingvellir, Iceland. The waterfall lies a little to the north of the Althing site.

CHAPTER | FIVE

EVERYDAY LIFE

THE SCANDINAVIAN COUNTRIES
IN THE VIKING AGE

Norway, Sweden and Denmark did not exist as clearly defined countries until the late Viking Age. The social and political organization could vary by region and the varying landscapes and different contacts with other peoples made the "Scandinavian" culture in the Viking Age less homogenous than it is often thought to be.

In Sweden, the regions of Götaland in the south, Svealand (central Sweden, Blekinge, part of the coastal region to the north and Öland) and Norrland in the north had their own leaders throughout the Viking Age. The island of Gotland was practically independent from the Scandinavian mainland. Through its offshore location in the Baltic Sea, the island had a distinctly individual culture. There is, for instance, the unique type of memorial stones, albeit related to the runestones of mainland Scandinavia: the Gotlandic picture stones. The jewellery also differs from that worn in the rest of Sweden. The northern half of Sweden, Finland and north Norway were the territory of the Sámi (previously also called Lapps). There were distinct similarities between certain beliefs and rituals of the Sámi and the Germanic Scandinavians. Archaeology and written sources show that there was extensive interaction between them that went beyond trading. Examples of cross-cultural marriages are known and graves with both Sámi and Nordic characteristics have been found.

The different regions had their own social and legal organization. The local *things* – assemblies held at set times at a central place, often a mound – were an important institution. This is where people would gather to discuss important decisions and pass laws.

The southern parts of modern Sweden, Skåne and Halland, were part of Denmark, which also included the part of northern Germany that is now Schleswig-Holstein. Jutland was the centre of a strong centralized power already in the eighth century. This is demonstrated by large-scale defences and infrastructures such as a series of fortresses, the Danevirke earthwork ramp and the Kanhave canal, which allowed ships to pass from one side of the island of Samsø to the other. Denmark had close contacts with the Frisians, Saxons and the larger Frankish Empire and later also with England.

Of Norway, only the southern part, coastal region and the fjords were inhabited. The first time the different parts were united under one ruler, King Harald Fairhair, was in *c.* AD 880. His death was followed by unstable successors, rebelling *jarls* (nobles) and periods of subjugation under Danish rule, which disrupted this unification again. Norway looked distinctly westwards and there was cultural interaction with the British Isles and, of course, the Icelandic colony.

In Denmark, people mostly lived together in villages, but there were single farmsteads too. The farms and villages were generally self-supporting and any surplus produce could be

traded for luxury items or silver. The settlement pattern was similar in the fertile plains of Västergötland in Sweden and the valleys in southern Norway. In the Swedish Mälarvalley, however, there were mainly single farmsteads, just as in the less fertile mountainous areas of Norway and Swedish Norrland.

The different regions had their own social and legal organization. At this time law was passed on orally, but some runic inscriptions give us a glimpse: at Oklunda, a man called Gunnar recorded by carving in a rock that he sought sanctuary at a *vi* (an assembly site where law was administered or a cult site) after committing, and admitting to, a crime. The oldest evidence we have for a Viking Age legal system is the Forsa rune ring from Hälsingland in Sweden. This ring has been hanging from a church door since the Middle Ages, but in the early Viking Age it had a different function. The ninth-century runic inscription proclaims what fines were payable if the *vi* was not maintained properly. That this law is referred to as being "of the people" and not, for example, issued by a king, indicates that there were ancient laws of the land that would apply to the people of a certain region.

Iceland was settled by Scandinavians, mainly from Norway, but also from Britain and Ireland, from *c.* AD 870 onwards. As we have seen (see page 34), they met Irish hermits there, but these men left at the arrival of the Norsemen and there does not seem to have been much cultural interaction. With nearly three-quarters of Iceland covered in glaciers and volcanic fields, only the coastal regions and the wider valleys in the south and south-west are fit for

LEFT Visitors walk along a cord road, made of logs, past a reconstructed Viking house at Hedeby, an area that is now in Germany but which was in Denmark in the Viking Age.

habitation and agriculture. The island was divided into districts and all free men had a vote in the regional assemblies. The districts were represented by the most powerful men – that is, the richest with the most land – at the yearly general assembly where justice was administered and decisions about the country were made more or less democratically.

SOCIAL STRUCTURE AND FAMILY LIFE

Most Viking Age Scandinavians were farmers. Even those who were Vikings in the true sense of the word had to come home to tend to their farms. Influence and power were connected to landownership and other wealth, which could be accumulated by raiding and trading during the seasons. This developed into a system where local chieftains or magnates "owned" an area with several farms, occupying the largest themselves. Place-names can clearly illustrate the social organization in the landscape, when they refer to the chieftain's or king's farm among other farms, assembly places, sacred groves, cult sites, smithies and so on.

Although not all farmers were also landowners, they were still free men. Other free men were merchants, craftsmen, hunters, fishers or poets, or a combination of any of these with farmer and/or Viking. Chieftains and kings held households, which could include bodyguards and stewards, and kings liked to employ one or more *skalds* (poets). Kings could call upon local chieftains to provide them with ships and men if needed for battles or expeditions. It could be a good career for young adventurous men to find fame and fortune in the retinue of a king or *jarl* before taking over the family farm.

The people lowest in rank were slaves. Slaves were mostly traded, but wealthy landowners could afford to have a slave work for them on their farm. A runestone in Hørning, Denmark, was raised by a man called Toki the smith, to commemorate Thorgisl who "gave him gold and freedom". This is a case of a slave who became a free man, well-off enough to commemorate his former master when he died.

Women played an important role in running the farm and household, since men could be away for most of the year. It is assumed that this role is symbolized by the iconic keys that are often found as part of a woman's attire. Women were fairly independent: they could own and inherit landed property and they could choose as well as divorce their husbands. Several written sources mention a woman called Aud the Deep-minded, who went to Iceland as one of the early settlers in the late ninth century to claim land after her husband's death. There are several extremely rich Viking Age female burials, testifying that women could be as highly placed as men, sometimes perhaps even higher. The most famous of these graves is the Oseberg ship burial, which was more impressive than any male burial in that region (see picture page 88). Two women were buried in the large ship, accompanied by a wealth of grave goods, including richly carved sleighs, an elaborately decorated wagon, imported silks and the famous tapestries. The grave had been disturbed (probably robbed, for there were no precious metals left) and any clues as to the relation between the younger and the older woman have been lost. Other pre-Christian burials, together with written sources, indicate that Viking Age women could also be cult leaders and prophetesses. Towards the later Viking Age, some women – like men – commissioned runestones to commemorate husbands, sons and daughters. From these inscriptions we also read that they were proud

ABOVE An employee at Hedeby, Germany, dressed in authentic Viking clothes, stands in front of one of the reconstructed houses.

Christians, who had bridges and causeways built and went on pilgrimage.

Among kings and chieftains it was common to have a son fostered by another family. This was a good way to forge and strengthen diplomatic bonds between families. Otherwise children were prepared for their future roles in society at home. Much of what children played with would have been made from natural materials such as wood, bone and cloth. None of these survive very well, but some miniature objects have been found and these are interpreted as childrens' toys. There are wooden dolls, horses and ships and child-size wooden swords.

Adults also liked a good game. Gaming pieces for board games of different materials, quality and wealth have been found. One memorial stone from Sweden even has a depiction of two men sitting at the games table with their drinking horns. Another favourite pastime was probably sports. People from the highest social strata went hunting with birds for leisure. In the long, dark winter, people entertained each other by telling stories and reciting poetry.

LEFT Harald Fairhair, the king who united Norway in the ninth century, at sea with his warriors. His hair is unkempt and shaggy because he vowed not to comb his hair until he ruled over all of Norway. Illustration by Morris Meredith Williams.

THE VIKING BELIEFS AND RITUALS

BELOW Viking burials could be elaborate affairs. The richest people would be buried with a ship to carry them to the afterlife and many possessions, and the burial covered over by a large mound. The burial ritual itself could be an extended performance that lasted many days, and the mound would have become a landmark and a sign of ownership of the area.

Viking Age spirituality and beliefs were very much part of daily life, interwoven with all aspects of Viking culture. For a long time, a book compiled by Snorri Sturluson in the early thirteenth century was taken as a sort of bible of pagan Viking religion (see page 9), but this is now considered to be an outdated approach. Although Snorri's *Edda* contains a compilation of stories about Viking gods and heroes and a general introduction to Viking Age mythology, he tells these stories as part of the broader purpose of the book: as reference and instruction for poets to retain the art of skaldic poetry (see page 103). Many of the *kennings*, or circumlocutions, that are used in skaldic poetry describe things or people with reference to these mythological and legendary stories. Snorri wanted to stimulate young poets to keep the old skaldic art alive,

so knowledge of these stories was as important for understanding and composing the poetry as knowledge of the intricate metres and rhyme-schemes, which he also explains.

The *Edda* contains tales about Odin (see page 9), Thor, Frey, Freyja and other gods, giants, and trolls. Snorri also presents a history of Viking mythology and a detailed description of the mythological world, with different realms for gods, men, giants, and an underworld, all centred round the tree of life. This is very much influenced by how the Christian religion was presented, which Snorri, as a learned Christian scholar, was familiar with. This reconstructed mythology does not reflect the place of the Viking Age beliefs in daily life. We must look to other sources such as burial customs, place-names and runestones to clarify and complete the picture. Snorri writes about Odin as the main god, but in Sweden, for instance, there are many more place-names containing the element "thor" while many finds have been made of amulets that take the form of small Thor's hammers. A handful of runestones also call upon this god to consecrate or protect the monument (or possibly the family involved in raising it). Clearly, not every god played the same role throughout Viking Age Scandinavia.

ABOVE A view of the interior of a reconstructed Viking Age house at L'Anse aux Meadows. The layout is typical of houses throughout Scandinavia in this period. In the centre is a fire pit. People would sit and sleep on the setts (benches) on either side of the central fire. There was little privacy in a Viking Age house. Everyone lived, ate and slept within the same space.

There was also an enormous diversity in the Viking Age burial practices. In pre-Christian times, most of those given a funeral were cremated, although some were buried. A variety of objects and animals could be buried with either the ashes and bones or the complete body. The grave itself could vary from a simple hole in the ground to a structure best described as an underground chamber. The way burials were marked varies too – from mounds to stone settings in the shape of the outline of a ship. The description by the Arab traveller Ibn Fadlan of a chieftain's funeral among the Viking Rus is an important source for the kinds of ritual that were performed at these occasions (see page 34). The preparation, construction and execution of burials could take a long time. Recent research explores how the placing of objects in graves and the ritual slaughtering of the animals were part of performing "funerary drama". Interestingly, though some rites seem to be linked to the social position of the deceased and the time they lived in, other customs appear to be specific for an individual local community or village.

Rituals and beliefs came into play not only when dealing with the dead; they were also very much a part of daily life. For instance, *norns* that could influence a person's fate and spirits that dwelled in natural

features had to be dealt with on a daily basis. For men going into battle, other beings became important, such as Odin's *valkyries*. There were people who specialized in interacting with the spiritual world of gods and other invisible beings. These sorcerers and sorceresses were also called upon to influence and resolve domestic affairs and issues in wider society.

MEMORY AND WRITTEN RECORD: POETRY, LAW AND RUNES

We call the language of the Vikings Old Norse, but there were substantial regional variations in the language that was spoken in Scandinavia. These versions of Old Scandinavian grew further and further apart during the Viking Age, but people from different parts of Scandinavia could still understand each other. The variations in spoken languages are also reflected in the runic writings of the later Viking Age.

Runes were in use as a writing system in Scandinavia from *c.* AD 200. They were used by Germanic peoples all over Europe, including Anglo-Saxon runes in England, but they remained in use the longest in Scandinavia. Like the Roman alphabet, each runic character represents one or more sounds from the spoken language. The rune-row is called the Futhark, named after the first five runes (the th-sound is represented by the þ-rune). In the early Viking Age, the Scandinavian rune-row underwent a reform. By the beginning of the eighth century, the Older Futhark, which consisted of 24 runic characters, had been transformed into a 16-rune rune-row, called the Younger Futhark. In the new system, the individual runes represented a larger number of sounds and, over time, different systems that allowed for more distinction were developed.

Although there were many conventions in how to carve a runic inscription, especially to be efficient with writing material, there was no standardized spelling and words were largely written how they sounded. Consequently, because how words were pronounced is reflected in how they were written, regional variations in the language can be identified. Individual carvers also adapted the system to suit their needs, and possible cases have even been identified where the spelling seems to reflect the carver's speech impediment.

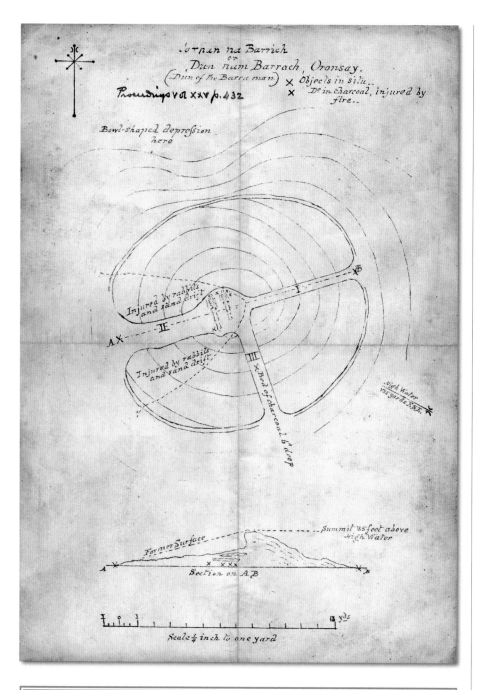

Viking Age runic writing consists of various types of text. Many inscriptions have survived on the iconic Viking Age stone monuments called runestones. These memorial inscriptions generally state who had the monument made in memory of whom and often information is added about lands that were owned by the deceased (possibly as claim to inheritance), expeditions, battles or pilgrimages they were involved in, or they mention that a causeway or road was constructed as part of the monument. Some runestones explicitly record the Christianization of certain areas, and many of the eleventh-century runestone inscriptions end with a Christian prayer for the soul of the commemorated. The majority of the runestones from the later period are also decorated with a Christian cross. At the same time there is a handful of runestones that invoke the god Thor to consecrate or protect the monument or that are decorated with a Thor's hammer.

Another common genre of runic inscription from the Viking Age consists of names on objects. This can be the name of the owner, of the producer, and sometimes of the object itself. Sometimes they added protective phrases – for example, against theft as on a copper box for storing scales found in Sigtuna in Sweden.

Because of their angular shape, runes were also very good for carving in wood and bone and this is how less monumental messages were exchanged. From the early medieval town of Bergen an enormous number of runic sticks – pieces of wood with runic inscriptions – have survived. Among the messages are official letters about politics and affairs as well as secret love letters and exchanges of glee about rude graffiti. Some of the more official letters use phrases that were common in the letters and charters of medieval Europe. Although a very small number of runic sticks have survived from Viking Age Hedeby,

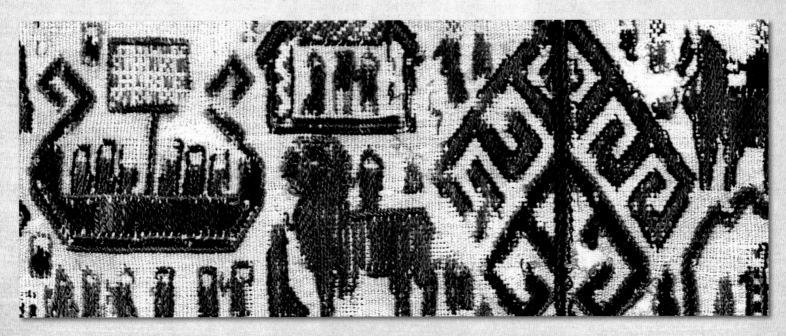

there is not enough comparable material from the Viking towns to conclude that the runic script was used for administrative and informal writing to the same extent as later in the medieval towns.

A common misconception is that runes were considered magic characters in the Viking Age. This misunderstanding seems to stem from the fact that many of the inscriptions in the Older Futhark have a ritual character and a connection between Odin and runes in mythology. Also in the Viking Age a rune-carver could, for instance, invoke Thor in an inscription on a memorial stone. This, however, does not make the runic script itself any more magical than writing a spell in our modern Roman alphabet would. To those who could not read the runes, the symbols may have had a mystic character and we do not know how much of the population could read runes. Still, in the Viking Age runic writing was mainly used on memorial stones and objects to record and boost ownership, provenance and purpose and only to a lesser extent to invoke certain powers, Christian as well as pagan.

Most information was transmitted not in written form, however, but orally. News travelled by word of mouth and lawspeakers played an important role in the Scandinavian legal system. These officials had as their main task to remember the law codes and recite these every year when judgement was to be passed at the assembly.

In this largely oral society, story-telling and reciting of poetry were important. Many of the mythological poems that were recorded onto vellum in the Middle Ages had their roots in Viking poems; these are called the Eddic poems. Another type of poetry is more about current events, praises kings and leaders and records the outcome of battles. These poems were composed by professional (court) poets, *skalds*, whose names are often transmitted with their verses as they were quoted as sources in medieval sagas. The *skalds* used an extremely intricate poetic form with a strict metre and complex poetic language such as *kennings*. This tight poetic form ensured accurate transmission of the content, because the one cannot be changed without corrupting the other. Skaldic poetry is not only about recording and transmitting information correctly; there is, for example, also love poetry. Using the skaldic metre and diction both correctly and originally was a challenge that made the poets highly appreciated artists.

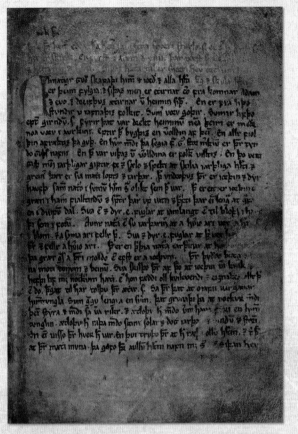

The Edda of Snorri Sturluson
in the Codex Uppsaliensis

Snorri's Edda was a manual for poetry written by the Icelandic scholar and poet Snorri Sturluson in the early thirteenth century. Snorri was concerned that the knowledge to understand Viking Age poetry was being lost, because the poetic language relied heavily on allusion to pagan mythology, which was not being passed on in Christian society. Therefore he collected together examples of poetry and the stories from mythology into one place. He also discussed the technicalities of writing poetry in the Norse style. Most of our knowledge about Norse mythology is gleaned from his work. The pages here show the Prologue, in which Snorri explores the origins of Norse mythology and draws parallels with other religions.

ART AND CRAFTS

Vikings not only appreciated well-wrought verse, they are also known for their love of artistic decoration and skill in producing beautiful objects. From the late eighth century to the mid-twelfth century the Oseberg, Borre, Jelling, Mammen, Ringerike and Urnes art styles – named after the finding places of significant objects – succeeded each other with, of course, a notable degree of overlap and regional variation. The Viking Age Scandinavian art styles are characterized by interlacing zoomorphic motifs, which partly goes back to a pan-Germanic style of animal ornament. In the subsequent Scandinavian styles the "ribbon-animal", (long ribbons ending in an animal head), "gripping-beast" and "Great Beast" (a creature similar to a dragon), make up the various phases of animal ornament. Other popular pictorial elements were naturalistic or stylized human faces or full-body human figures. There are also narrative scenes that can combine several human figures, animals, ships, buildings or other objects. Some of the recurring figures and scenes from Viking art can be identified. The female figures with trailing dresses and often a drinking horn have been interpreted as *valkyries*. We can recognize Sigurd the Dragonslayer a number of times, as well as Thor fishing for the Midgard Serpent and possibly Odin at Ragnarök. Christian motifs and scenes were also popular. For instance, small cross pendants with a crucified Christ were produced and the large runestone at Jelling, on which King Harald Bluetooth proclaims he has Christianized all of Denmark (see page 113), is decorated with a large figure of Christ in a crucified position. Other common motifs and scenes include armed men and riders on horseback in hunting or warrior context, crewed ships, processions, figures that have human as well as animalistic characteristics, birds of prey, dogs and wolves.

These motifs and scenes were used to decorate a wide range of objects and materials, from brooches and helmets to ships and from metalwork and wood to wall hangings. In particular, Thor's hammers and valkyrie figurines were cast as amulets. There are also small statuettes that may represent gods: Frey from Rällinge, Sweden; Thor from Eyrarland, Iceland; Freja from Lejre, Denmark; and an armed *valkyrie* from Hårby, Denmark.

The specialized craftsmen who produced these decorated objects and their plain counterparts used a variety of techniques. Archaeological finds show that there was a market for mass-produced objects as well as for unique masterpieces, presumably manufactured for a specific person.

The working of wood and iron, both materials that generally tended to be locally available,

PREVIOUS PAGES
An aerial view of reconstructed Viking houses at L'Anse aux Meadows in Newfoundland. The houses are built of turf, as they were in Iceland where wood was scarce.

LEFT The late-tenth-century Karlevi runestone in Öland, Sweden, is the only monument to combine the medium of stone with the medium of skaldic verse with its tight metre and kennings. The inscription reads:
This stone is placed in memory of Sibbi the good, Fuldarr's son, and his retinue placed on ...
He lies concealed, he who was followed by the greatest deeds (most men knew that), a chieftain (battle-tree of [the Goddess] Þrúðr) in this howe;
Never again shall such a battle-hardened sea-warrior (Viðurr-of-the-Carriage of [the Sea-king] Endill's mighty dominion (= God of the vessels of the sea)), rule unsurpassed over land in Denmark.

OPPOSITE The eleventh-century runestone at Altuna, Sweden (LEFT) and the carved stone at Gosforth, England (RIGHT), are both decorated with Thor fishing for the Midgard Serpent. This indicates that the myths brought by the Norse settlers were known and appreciated in England. The monuments contain details that match the different versions of the story that have been written down. On the Swedish monument, the god is depicted with his hammer Mjölnir. The force of his struggle with the monster on his fishing line is such that his foot goes through the bottom of the boat. On the Gosforth fishing stone, Thor is accompanied by a giant, who cuts the line when Thor is about to heave the serpent out of the waters.

was very important for constructing ships, buildings, weapons, utensils and the tools to make these things. Smaller household items and personal objects like needles, spindle whorls and combs were carved out of antler or bone. The rarer material of whale bone could be used to fashion larger decoratively carved plaques that were probably used as smoothing boards.

Horn is a softer material that does not have to be carved, but can be cut and moulded into objects such as spoons. Horns could also be used to make the iconic Viking drinking vessels. Drinking glasses were not produced locally, but were imported as exclusive luxury items. There was, however, a Scandinavian glass-working tradition for producing brightly coloured beads out of imported broken glass. Pottery was also imported – in particular, highly decorated jugs from the Rhineland – but simple pottery, such as bowls, was produced locally. These objects could also be made out of soapstone.

Leather must have been commonly produced and used, especially for shoes. However, little of this survives other than remains of leatherworking workshops in towns. Textiles for clothing and household use were mainly produced locally too. Wool and flax were spun by hand into threads that were woven into fabric. Clothing was often very colourful and decorated in various ways, by dyeing and applying intricately woven bands or embroidery.

The Vikings produced a very wide range of jewellery. Silver, gold and bronze were made into arm rings and finger rings, pendants

and brooches. The techniques used include casting, carving or stamping the metals, which could then be embellished by applying niello, filigree and granulation. Foreign trinkets and coins could be incorporated into the jewellery, especially in the strings of beads and pendants that hung between the brooches on women's outfits. It was mainly through jewellery that people expressed their regional identity and social standing. The same techniques were used to decorate high-status armour, weapons and horse equipment.

VIKING FARMS, LONGHOUSES AND TOWNS

The reconstructions of Viking Age houses are mainly based on archaeological excavations. Anything above the ground has left far fewer traces than those parts that were dug into the earth. However, the positions of post-holes outline the curve of the walls and indicate the size of the building and the number of internal supporting pillars. This information can be used to calculate, for instance, the height of the building. The remains of fire pits and internal structures indicate which types of activity took place in the different parts of the house. Modern reconstructions have been important for finding out about air circulation and smoke-holes. The building materials – timber, turf and stone – varied regionally, depending on availability, but the shape of the farmhouses was pretty much uniform throughout Scandinavia. The size of the

houses also varies and this reflects to a certain extent how they were used.

The early Viking Age longhouses housed dwelling space and animal byre under the same roof. In the course of the Viking Age, however, the internal structure of the farmhouses changed. The side walls carried more of the roof's weight so the internal pillars disappeared. The byre became a separate building and it became more common to have smaller buildings for specific purposes, such as smithying and weaving. The longhouses had a large rectangular hearth in the centre which was used for heating and cooking. Benches along the walls provided place for sitting, working and sleeping. Particularly large longhouses could contain a permanent space for feasting, ceremonies or other public gatherings, often called a hall. But smaller farmhouses could also fulfil this function on occasion. In relatively close proximity to the farmhouse buildings, archaeologists find domestic waste deposits and burials, the contents of which can provide additional information about life on that particular farm.

Most people lived in small agricultural settlements, but early towns where people made a living from producing and trading non-agricultural goods began to emerge. The development of trade routes stimulated the further growth of early towns on strategic locations, such as Ribe and Hedeby in Denmark, Kaupang in Norway and Birka in Sweden. Town houses were smaller rectangular houses with separate workshops and they were often situated along streets leading to the harbour, on individually fenced plots. The towns themselves tended to have a defence structure and kings or chieftains were involved in guaranteeing the safety of the inhabitants and visiting merchants. The quality of goods on offer attracted many foreign merchants, such as Frisians, Saxons, Slavs, Eastern Europeans and Spanish Arabs. This is illustrated by the burial of some of them at Hedeby and Birka and, of course, by the goods and coins that they brought. The towns functioned as marketplaces for the surrounding area, on which they relied for agricultural supplies. The economic significance of towns translated to political importance, making it desirable for chieftains and kings and the Christian Church to have a strong hold over them. Later towns – such as Schleswig and Roskilde in Denmark, Sigtuna and Visby in Sweden and Trondheim in Norway – might have had additional functions as assembly sites, religious or administrative centres with, for instance, kings' mints. Also in areas of Norse settlement abroad, there were towns with a distinctly Scandinavian character and Scandinavian street names, such as Dublin (see page 73), York, and Lincoln. In addition to the real towns – with a permanent population of people living from manufacture and trade – there was a large network of trading posts or seasonal markets (*emporia*) which extended beyond the Viking homelands and the areas of Norse settlement. To the east, for example, along the river Volga, trading posts were founded by Vikings at Staraja Ladoga and Novgorod.

CHAPTER | SIX

THE END OF THE VIKING AGE

THE COMING OF CHRISTIANITY: MISSIONARIES, KINGS AND WOMEN

In the late Viking Age, Christianity came to Scandinavia, but Vikings had known about the Christian religion for a long time, as the rest of Europe had been Christian since the early Viking Age. Vikings first became familiar with Christianity abroad, and Christian merchants frequented the Scandinavian trading centres. Vikings regularly chose to be baptized on expeditions when trade or diplomatic contacts were at stake. They were not exactly converted: Christ, the holy trinity and the saints were simply added to the existing system of beliefs. Scandinavians who settled abroad, like many did in England, Scotland and Ireland, adopted the Christian religion there.

Frankish, Anglo-Saxon and Icelandic sources record the Christianization of Scandinavia, each from a different perspective. Archaeological evidence suggests that there was a long transitional period in Scandinavia during which the pagan and Christian cultures existed side by side. The runestones show, and sometimes specifically state, when Christianity became important in a region. Some runestones mention that an area had converted to Christianity while others say that an individual had gone on pilgrimage. Many inscriptions include a Christian prayer for the soul of the dead and often, especially on eleventh-century runestones, the decoration includes carvings of Christian crosses.

Missionaries had come to Scandinavia from the eighth century onwards. The Frankish emperor Louis the Pious supported the exiled Danish king Harald Klak, who had converted to Christianity, and helped him onto the Danish throne twice (AD 812–814 and AD 819–827), sending missionaries with him. Ansgar, later archbishop of Hamburg-Bremen, was the most successful of these. He also went to Birka in Sweden. The results of Ansgar's mission in Denmark did, however, not reach further than south Jutland and it was not until King Harald Bluetooth (who reigned c. AD 958–986) that Denmark was Christianized. King Harald was pressured by the Frankish emperor Otto to convert. Bishoprics were already established in several of his royal power centres and it is clear that King Harald's conversion and his Christianization campaign were strategic decisions in order to consolidate his power. After his conversion, King Harald changed the royal burial monument at Jelling. He built a church there and placed, between the two mighty burial mounds, an imposing runestone. The monument is decorated with a lion and an image of an heroic Christ. The inscription commemorates Harald's parents and states that he "made all of Denmark Christian".

In Norway, Harald Fairhair (who reigned

AD 872–930) realized that Christianity was important to unite Norway and establish good international contacts. He had his son fostered by the Christian King Aethelstan in England and subsequent generations of kings tried to convert Norway with Anglo-Saxon support before Olaf Haraldson (who reigned 1015–1028 and later became St Olaf) succeeded through a combination of evangelization, legislation and force. The local chieftains resisted conversion because Christianity was better suited for a centralized power structure than the old faith. Vikings were happy to be baptized abroad for diplomatic reasons, but living in a Christian country would diminish their independence.

Iceland was an independent republic, but still bound to Norway through family ties and trade. The Norwegian kings had enough power to influence the Christianization there. *Íslendingabók*, the twelfth-century Icelandic chronicle, tells us that it was decided to adopt Christianity at the *Althing* (national assembly) in the year AD 999–1000. It is likely that the Norwegian King Olaf Tryggvasson put a lot of pressure behind this decision, precisely because it gave him more influence over the island. The colony in Greenland seems to have been Christian from an early time; shortly after the Vikings arrived there in *c.* AD 985 a church was built in Brattahlíð.

The conversion period took the longest in Sweden. The first Christian king was Olof Skötkonung, who reigned AD 995–1022, but

FAR LEFT A silver penny of Cnut struck at York.

LEFT A stone mould used by a Viking smith to cast both crosses and Thor's hammers. This illustrates a very pragmatic approach to the co-existence of the Christian religion and pre-Christian beliefs.

OPPOSITE The cemetery at Jelling Church, Denmark. In the background is the grave mound of King Gorm the Old, which was raised in the late tenth century. The larger – and younger – of the two Jelling runestones that stand outside the church record how King Harald Bluetooth brought Christianity to Denmark. Harald is supposed to have moved the bones of his father Gorm from the pagan burial mound into the original church that stood on this site.

Olof's successors did not have sufficient power to Christianize the whole of Sweden until the thirteenth century. The German medieval chronicler Adam of Bremen, writing *c.* 1070, mentions a large pagan cult in Old Uppsala. He never visited this area and his story is exaggerated, but archaeological material suggests that customs related to the old beliefs were indeed practised for a long time there. The multitude of eleventh-century Christian runestones that were erected in Uppland and Södermanland, however, show that there simultaneously were many Christians there.

In the late Viking Age, the Christian kings and the Church together introduced Christian laws and regulations. Conversion was no longer just accepting the new religion, but also included denouncing the old beliefs, customs and rituals. In this phase of Christianization women played an important role, as they were the ones who supervised the daily running of the household, including the spiritual matters.

The conversion of the Nordic countries also meant many changes in the daily life. Offerings to the gods and spirits became taboo and burial rites changed. Strict regulations with regard to marriage, sexuality and diet were introduced. The days for feasting and fasting that constituted the Christian religious year changed the yearly routine. Finally, the hierarchical structure of the Christian religion and Church and the introduction of the concepts of sin and redemption influenced the Viking mentality and world-view.

Alongside these changes there was a significant continuity between the old and the new religion. Aspects of the Christian faith were explained to appeal to, and connect with, the Norse culture and mentality. For instance, a connection was made between the Germanic hero Sigurd the Dragonslayer and Christ as conqueror of evil. Continuity was also created between old customs and traditions and the Christian feasts, and between places of worship and power by building churches at cult or assembly sites.

SCANDINAVIA BECOMES PART OF EUROPE: THE VIKING AGE ENDS

The establishment of the Scandinavian countries as monarchies with centralized power went hand in hand with the Christianization of the Viking homelands. The first Scandinavian churches were established in trading centres, where there was already some familiarity with the Christian religion, by Frankish and Anglo-Saxon missionaries. Later, when the Scandinavian kings had converted and were Christianizing their realms to increase their power and strengthen diplomatic relations with rulers elsewhere in Europe, they had churches built too. They often chose locations that were already important political centres or cult sites, such as Jelling and Old Uppsala. The authority of such places reflected on the Christian institute and it was simultaneously a clear power statement by the king. Local magnates followed and had churches built on their estates, initially

for private use. The first churches in Scandinavia were made of wood. The iconic Norwegian stave churches were produced into the thirteenth century (see picture, page 112 of Fagusnes, Borgund in Norway), while from the twelfth century onwards stone churches were starting to be built in Denmark and parts of Sweden. The Scandinavian churches and monasteries fell under the Archbishop of Hamburg-Bremen until the first Scandinavian archbishopric was established in Lund in 1104. In the course of the twelfth century Norway and Sweden also got their own archbishoprics, recognizing them as independent Christian states.

From 1016–1035 King Cnut ruled what was known as the Danelaw in England (see page 59). From there, he also took up the Danish throne and took measures to consolidate his Anglo-Scandinavian empire. He married Emma of Normandy, Aethelred's widow, and continued his laws and taxes. Cnut also had similar coins minted for England and Denmark, emphasizing

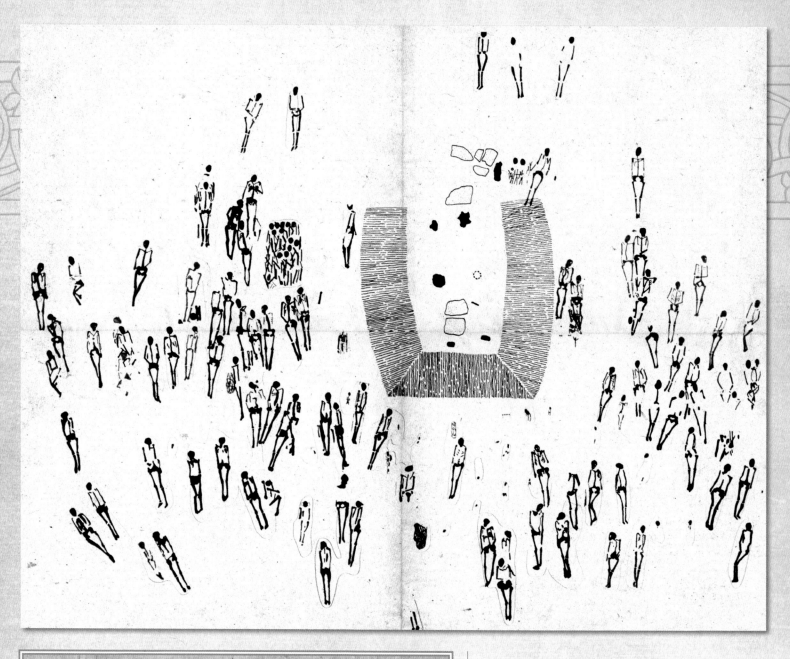

This drawing shows the locations of the graves around the church at Brattahlið (Qassiarsiuk), Greenland. This is a Christian burial ground that surrounds the church that Eirik the Red's wife, Thjodhild, had built, while Eirik the Red was still a pagan. The skeletons in the graveyard were all buried in the Christian fashion with their heads to pointing west. Analysis of the bones shows that the average life expectancy here was 35 years and that most people did not live past 45 years of age. Several of the skeletons had head injuries consistent with being hit by a sword or axe, and one had a knife blade between its ribs.

the extent of his realm. Towards the end of his reign Cnut was a strong presence in medieval European politics, also ruling Norway and parts of Sweden at some point.

This carefully forged Anglo-Scandinavian empire did not last long after Cnut's death in 1035. In 1042 Edward the Confessor, Aethelred's son, who had been exiled in his mother's native Normandy for 25 years, claimed the English throne. When King Edward died in 1066, King Harald Hardrada of Norway, an ambitious Viking known as "the Ruthless", prepared a campaign to conquer England. He was supported by the Earl of Orkney and the exiled Earl of Northumbria and the attack came as a surprise for the English King Harold Godwinson. Nevertheless, Godwinson raised an army larger and more quickly than Harald expected. On 25 September 1066, a fierce battle at Stamford Bridge took place and Harald was defeated. The *Anglo-Saxon Chronicle* tells us the Norwegians arrived with a fleet of some 300 ships, of which they needed only 24 to take the survivors of the battle home.

King Harold Godwinson of England only had a little time to recover, for William of Normandy, a descendant of the Viking ruler Rollo (see page 86), had similar ambitions to Harald Hardrada. If the winds had been different that September, history might have taken a different course. Harald and William had prepared their fleets at the same time, but William could not sail out until after the battle at Stamford Bridge, at which the English army suffered severe losses. When they faced the Norman army just over a fortnight later near Hastings on 14 October, King Harold nevertheless put up a fierce defence. William's host, however, was stronger and after his victory at Hastings the rest of England was conquered quickly. The story of the victory was embroidered on a commemorative tapestry in Bayeux, probably ordered by bishop Odo, who was William's half-brother. The Norman conquest was the end of Scandinavian rule over England. In subsequent years, attempts to reclaim parts of England failed because the Scandinavian armies were too depleted after decades of internal power struggles and by Harald Hardrada's final campaign. The descendants of the Viking settlers in England had in the meantime integrated in the cultural melting pot of the Anglo-Saxons.

King Magnus Barelegs of Norway (who reigned 1093–1103) brought the independent earldoms and kingdoms in the Northern and Western Isles (Orkney, the Hebrides and the Isle of Man), most ruled by descendants of the independent Viking settlers, under Norwegian rule. In subsequent centuries, however, the various islands changed hands between Manx, Scottish and Norwegian kings, until they were all, with Orkney last, eventually sold or mortgaged to the Scottish kings in the course of the twelfth to fifteenth centuries.

The Scandinavian countries never were truly feudal states. But, following on from the new centralized power structure crafted with the introduction of Christianity, the tithe system (already in practice in the rest of medieval Europe) was introduced to Denmark in the twelfth century. Taxes were collected and obligations to Church and king became connected to landownership. The kings granted lands in exchange for military services. Soon, the same development took place in Norway and Sweden. In the thirteenth century, the unstable political situation in Iceland gave the Norwegian king Håkon IV the opportunity to subject the republic to his rule. The profitable Greenland colony fell under his reign too. In the following centuries a combination of climate change and new sources for the luxury goods like ivory and furs that had been exported from Greenland led to the abandonment of the colony and thus the gateway across the Atlantic to the far west.

The conditions that created the opportunities for raiding and taking lands for settlements had changed. The surplus of men and the element of surprise had gone and the advantage of having innovative fast boats was not enough. Instead, the Scandinavian countries had established themselves as worthy partners in the political, religious and trade networks of the medieval world.

CHAPTER | SEVEN

THE VIKING LEGACY

THE LINGUISTIC, GENETIC AND CULTURAL INHERITANCE

By the end of the Viking Age, the Scandinavians who had settled in the British Isles had been mixing with the people there for a couple of generations. The result was a distinct Norse influence in regions where many Vikings had settled, such as the former Danelaw and the Northern Isles. We can still see this in, for example, the dialects and place-names in those regions. Norn is an extinct language closely related to the Old Norse of the Vikings settlers. It was spoken in the Northern Isles and the far north of Scotland and declined only in the late fourteenth century when it was superseded by Scots. Norn continued to be spoken up to the eighteenth century and certain Norn, as well as Old Norse, influences still remain in the Orkney dialect. Present-day English is also partly made up of words originating from Old Norse:

Do you go *berserk* with *anger* when your *freckle-nosed husband* eats the *eggs* you need to bake a *cake* for your *guests*? Then you speak Old Norse!

The landscape in the Scandinavian homelands is scattered with archaeological material from the Viking Age. There are remains of buildings, cemeteries (most well preserved is Lindholm høje, which is north of the city of Aalborg in Denmark), assembly sites (the largest is Thingvellir in Iceland) and many runestones, especially in central Sweden. The Viking heritage is also exploited in the Scandinavian tourist industry and is often expressed in local arts and crafts. This can be in a reinvented form, where historical accuracy is less important than the creation and expression of a cultural identity.

Many products and companies choose a Viking-inspired name or logo. The connotations of "Viking" in this context are clearly positive. Apparently Vikings are perceived by the marketing industry as strong, bold, effective, innovative and independent, but also, maybe more surprisingly, as reliable. Viking Lines Ferries and NorthLink Ferries, the first named after the Vikings and the second with a Viking as their trademark, both create a connection between their ferry service and the seamanship of the Vikings.

The strong sentiment connected to identifying Viking heritage also lies behind the interest in participating in genetic studies. Major academic research into Viking ancestry has been undertaken using DNA sampling. In combination with information from archaeology, surnames and place-names, it is now possible to draw conclusions about the history of Viking immigration in a region. This research confirms, for instance, that the English Wirral Peninsula and west Lancashire were heavily settled by Norse Vikings. A Norse ancestry can be recognized with a fair amount of certainty, but Danish Viking can not yet be distinguished from Anglo-Saxon control groups.

People in areas of previous Viking settlement are generally interested in or even celebrate

LEFT A still of Amalie
Materna (1844–1918)
as Brunnhilde in the
first performance of
Wagner's *Ring Cycle*,
which took place in
1876. This Austrian
soprano performed
as Brunnhilde from
Bayreuth to New York.

OPPOSITE Drangey,
Iceland, is an island
shaped like an arrow
pointing north. It is now
a bird sanctuary, but it
was once the hideout of
Grettir Asmundarsson, a
notorious outlaw. As told
in *Grettis saga*, Grettir
lived here for three years
with his brother, Illugi,
and his slave, Glaumr.

their Norse past. On Shetland, the yearly Upp Helly Aa fire festival combines a parade of men in fantasy uniforms with Viking elements with the burning of a specially built Viking ship (see picture on page 120 and pages 124–5). This particular tradition has its roots in the nineteenth century when unruly yuletide celebrations became a regulated festivity to which a flavour of a romanticized Viking history was added in the twentieth century. At roughly the same time in Normandy, in 1911, a historic festival celebrated the 1,000 years since the granting of land to Rollo "the Dane". In Russia,

the Viking legacy has been researched and celebrated only since the communist regime ended in the 1990s. Before that, history was dictated to be a purely Slavic affair, without any foreign contributions or positive involvement.

Also part of the cultural legacy of the Vikings are the fake artefacts created to illustrate, enhance or even invent a Viking past. One such example is the Kensington runestone from Minnesota in the USA, which still generates discussion about its provenance, despite having been identified as a nineteenth-century creation.

MEDIEVAL SAGAS

The medieval Icelanders also felt a strong connection with their Viking ancestors. Written down in this period were the famous Icelandic sagas, many of which take place in the Viking Age. This does not, however, mean they originated entirely *from* the Viking Age. They were written down from approximately 1150 onwards in the centres of religion and learning which had developed in medieval Iceland, such as Hólar, Skálholt, Haukadal and Oddi. The most famous sagas, however, were written in the thirteenth century and in a more secular setting, often with partly political motivations.

Scholars tend to group the sagas into several categories. The *fornaldarsögur* (legendary sagas) relate legends of ancestors from the ancient, mythical past. The *konungasögur* (sagas of kings) tell stories about the kings of Norway and the *Íslendingasögur* (sagas of Icelanders or family sagas) are mainly about prominent Viking Age Icelanders. The saga narratives tend to span several generations and the latter two types in particular include extensive genealogies for many of the characters, showing how they are related to each other and often to the medieval Icelandic families of the day.

Various aspects of the content and form of many sagas suggest that they are based on oral tradition. The *fornaldarsögur* contain or retell Eddic poems about mythical heroes. An example is the *Völsungasaga* about the hero Sigurd the Dragonslayer, the Völsungs and Gjukungs and the famously ill-fated Rhine gold. A collection of Eddic poems has also survived in a manuscript

LEFT A guizer at the Up Helly Aa festivities in Lerwick, Shetland, stands before the burning ship. The festival in its current form dates to the late nineteenth century.

called the *Codex Regius* and some of them are dated to the Viking Age. The kings' and family sagas are often based on the information recorded in skaldic poetry and many skaldic verses are quoted in these sagas. These poems were generally composed by *skalds* to praise a king. Because of their strict metre, rhyme scheme and particular vocabulary, these poems could be transmitted orally without changing much (see page 103). So a skaldic poem about a king was deemed to be an appropriate source for the writer of a saga about that particular king. Similarly, sagas about famous Viking *skalds*, such as the illustrious Egill Skallagrímsson (*Egil's saga*), contain poetry attributed to them.

Other types of sagas show that the medieval Icelanders were familiar with medieval European and classical literary traditions. There were romances and chivalric tales, translated and retold from Middle English and French – for instance, about Sir Arthur and the Knights of the Round Table and Charlemagne. There were saints' lives and sagas about bishops. There were translations of classical historical works and Icelandic medieval chronicles. These types of saga (and their inspiration) have also influenced the more indigenous *fornaldarsögur*, *konungasögur* and *Íslendingasögur*.

Although some kings' and family sagas are firmly rooted in the genealogies, landscape and historical events, they should not be taken as historical sources. We do not know, after all, precisely how

ABOVE This is an image of Icelandic houses as seen by William Morris on one of his trips to Iceland in the 1870s. Morris was an English textile designer, artist and writer who developed a love for Iceland on his travels. Morris was the first to make many of the Icelandic sagas accessible in English.

OPPOSITE: The Codex Regius

The Icelandic thirteenth-century Codex Regius contains a large collection of Norse mythological and legendary poems, called the Poetic Edda. For many of the poems this manuscript is the only source. The poems were thus preserved in a thirteenth-century written form, but they go back to much older oral traditions, which can be shown through linguistic analysis and literary parallels.

oc er þv þeima siv bar hon hon hꜵnte z þo amelis ꜵþ m̄. er
h dryccr eg 4: H mli er sem fyrr v sigmd. h l. lꜵtv gꜵm
si þa sonr. Sinsiotli dcc. z varþ þegar dauþ. Sigmde bar
h langar leidir i þangt s z kom at fiorþi eino miovo ac
longo z v þar seþ er lidiþ z v er a. h baþ sigmd þar
op yncꜵbiv. er er sigmunde bar licr vt a scipt þa var
bꜵrt hlꜵbdr. kl. mli at sigmde scyldr vera f. iþa þ
biv. hꜵrl hvat vt scipino z hvarf þegar. Sigmde kor
dvalþiz lengi i þanmore irik1 borgh. siþ er h rece var. Jm
sigm. þa lvþ iy rꜵce l̄. c þes rices er h atte þar. Da rec h
hiꜵdisar d. eyluma kl. fra l̄. var sigvrþ. Sigmde kꜵr
fell i orosto fyr hvndigt. ff. Er hiꜵdis giptir þa alfr f.
hialprecs kl. Oc sigvrþ þar up i barne sco. Sigmde z allir
fyn hl voro langt v fram alla m̄ aþra vm afl yvoreoc
hug z alla at gervi. Sigvrþ v þa allra fimarstr z h cala
allir m̄ þ þann fyrþo v alla m̄ z m̄ z gafigastan h kn.
rip h. s. eyluma b. hiꜵdisar. h reþ londo z v allra maia
vitrastr z fra vis. Sig. reiþ er saman z com c hallar g
þis. Sig. v aþkende hꜵer. m̄. at mali ver f. hꜵillꜵi
fa nefndir geit. þa gꜵdi sig. h mall. z spyrr. Hvr byᴇir
lþ borg þar hvat þan þioþ kg begnat nꜵia. gpir hetir
ꜵvna stiꜵr fa er fastri reþ foldo z þegno. Er hꜵsler kg
heta ꜵandi mun fa gnir viþ me gga at mkia mall er
þarri þ okvnigr vil ec fnothga fvia gpi. Des mvn
glꜵde kg grim spyria hvr fa iþ te c malt ꜵr gpi. siᴇ
ec heter bꜵrn sigmdi er hiꜵdis c hilmiþ moþir. Da geit
geit gripi ar   fegia h er v ver okvþ hꜵin h er
ternsigr at alter fa vil fylᴇ fvþ þiy hria. Gᴇinᴇe ꜵ fa
la lᴇꜵena ꜵeriy z heilfar vel hilmi cominn. þic kv h fiᴇ
vi fonꜵn fyrn er þv geit tac v grana filiꜵo. Wꜵla na
mo z mat t hrala þa er raþpae recar yvrdvr frꜵdvm
er þv veir moþvr broþ tve mvn fiᴇþi fnvna eᴇi:
Dv minne iþ ba myrery vnd folo z hestr bꜵriy hvior
þꜵ ᴇvrvll aþ gꜵlli er gleyer y lugꜵ ter alter z rꜵþo
                                                          fpꜵer.

and what sources, foreign literary traditions and political agendas have influenced the story. Nor do we know how the compiler balanced their aims of entertaining, recording and instructing. However, the composition of the sagas and the place of these stories in the Icelandic narrative and manuscript tradition clearly reflect an interest in the Viking Age that is unique for medieval times. Above all, though, these narratives about moody, wise, heroic and treacherous characters, and their dealings with magic and monsters, their loves and losses, political intrigues and personal feuds are literary works in their own right.

Visitors to Iceland today can explore various saga landscapes. Saga tours provide us with the opportunity to get a taste of the Icelandic perception of the landscape as embedded with narrative. The famous *Njál's saga* is mainly set in the south of Iceland, while the protagonist of *Gísla saga* travelled widely in the Westfjords as an outlaw. Adventurous travellers can descend into Surtshellir, a cave formed by lava, which has been used as a hideout by outlaws since the Viking Age. It is mentioned in *Landnámabók* and a small number of sagas. Archaeological remains from the Viking Age, such as large quantities of animal bones and interior constructions, testify to its intensive use.

NATIONAL ROMANTICISM AND THE MYTH OF THE VIKING

From the sixteenth century onwards, people in Britain were interested in Anglo-Saxon history, viewing the Anglo-Saxon period as a golden age of freedom. The *Anglo-Saxon Chronicle* and other texts described the wars with the Vikings. There was no structured approach to investigating this period and much of the work undertaken was pure guesswork, which led to many sites being labelled as Viking without any real grounds for doing so. For example, the large number of earthworks around Britain were identified as Danish camps, though most pre-date the Viking Age. Some serious scholarship was attempted in the seventeenth century by scholars such as Thomas Bartholin and Ole Worm in Denmark and Olof Rudbeck in Sweden, while in Britain the eighteenth century saw a dramatic rise in interest in the Vikings. In fact, the earliest recorded use of the word Viking was 1807. However, it was the Victorian period that brought more serious attention to the Vikings and to some extent it is fair to say that the Victorians effectively invented the modern Viking.

The driving force for nineteenth-century interest in the Vikings was largely national romanticism. This was a period when nation states were being formed and the Vikings, with their vigorous activities, provided a vehicle for inventing national identities. To this end, people like Sir Walter Scott drew on Norse and Anglo-Saxon imagery to promote their own ideas about identity; in Scott's case this was a Scottish identity, of course. Images of noble, upright, seafaring Vikings, like the paintings of Friðjof by T H Robinson, similarly promoted an English identity. As a seafaring race, the English could identify with this sort of Viking.

The appearance of the Viking in fiction and art was matched by scholarly interest. Translations

of Old Norse works had appeared in the eighteenth century, but these came to English via Latin, because English scholars had not yet learnt Old Norse. From one of these comes the idea that Vikings drank from the skulls of their enemies. When, in one of his "Runic Odes" in 1748, Thomas Warton used the lines:

"Where luscious Wines for ever flow,
Which from the hollow Sculls we drain,
Of Kings in furious Combat slain."

he was perpetuating and increasing the audience for Magnús Ólafsson's Latin mistranslation of a *kenning* for "drinking horns" in the Old Norse poem *Krákumál*. Only in the mid-nineteenth century did English readers learn that Vikings had not, in fact, drunk from the skulls of their enemies.

As archaeological discoveries were made throughout the nineteenth century, knowledge about Vikings was expanded and better communications between Scandinavia and Britain enabled each to learn from the other. Scholars began to learn Old Norse and read the sagas in the original language, which improved on earlier misunderstandings. This did not hinder speculative efforts, though. There were still attempts to trace Queen Victoria's lineage back to Odin and to prove that the Princess of Wales was related to the great Danish king Harald Bluetooth.

Enthusiasm for the Vikings continued strongly into the twentieth century. As in the nineteenth century, people found the virtues they wanted in the Vikings, leading to a whole mythology of Vikingness that was used for both good and evil. In Nazi Germany, the Vikings were considered to be of the same blood as the Germans and the Viking myth was used to bolster Nazi ideology. In Russia, after the revolution, it was denied that the Vikings had ever influenced Russian culture or history at all.

In the present day, Vikings have been rehabilitated from these negative elements. The image of the plundering, pillaging Viking is still with us, but it is counterbalanced by greater awareness of the other aspects of Viking life, such as the technologies they used and their poetry. The Viking legacy speaks to us all in different ways, but it cannot be denied that it is present and enduring, however it is perceived.

OVERLEAF: Flateyjarbok

Most of the Icelandic sagas about Norse Kings are collected in this fourteenth-century manuscript. The first page shows the end of the *Saga of Eirik the Far-farer*, who is supposed to have travelled to Byzantium and India. The red text with the illuminated initial H annouces that the *Saga of Olaf Tryggvason* begins here. The picture is of Harald Fairhair and the saga begins with a short history of his reign. The second page describes the birth and baptism of Olaf. The illuminated initial shows his mother Astrid in the bed with the infant Olaf.

BIBLIOGRAPHY

The further reading recommended here has been chosen on the basis of readily available English language books. Those that want more information will find their bibliographies useful.

TRANSLATIONS OF IMPORTANT WORKS

Translations of the Icelandic sagas provide a useful starting point for reading Old Norse literature. These three important sagas cover the main topics that interested medieval Icelanders. *Njal's saga* is widely agreed to be the pinnacle of saga writing with love, vengeance and courtroom drama being major themes in the text. *Laxdæla saga* may have had a female author. It centres on a love triangle in Laxardal with fatal consequences. *Egil's saga* tells the story of the unruly Icelandic poet Egill Skallagrímsson, whose encounters with people like Erik Bloodaxe ensured that he never had a quiet life.

Cook, R. (trans.), *Njal's Saga* (London, 2001)
Kunz, K. (trans.), *The Saga of the People of Laxardal and Bolli Bollason's Tale* (London, 2008)
Svanhildur Óskarsdóttir (trans.), *Egil's saga* (London, 2004)

The Poetic Edda contains stories of both gods and heroes, and contains gnomic wisdom that highlights the attitudes and morals of the Vikings.

Larrington, C. (trans.), *The Poetic Edda* (Oxford, 2014)
Orchard, A. (trans.), *The Elder Edda: A Book of Viking Lore* (London, 2011)

In the thirteenth century Snorri Sturluson wrote down stories from Norse myth as part of his manual of poetry, *The Prose Edda*. His *Heimskringla* is an important historical document that sheds light on Viking Age Norway.

Faulkes, A. (trans.) and Snorri Sturluson, *Edda* (London, 2005)
Hollander, L. (trans.) and Snorri Sturluson, *Heimskringla History of the Kings of Norway* (Austin, 2011)

Arab writers give us detailed contemporary descriptions of what Viking Rus looked like. A selection is included in this translation.

Lunde, P. and Stone, C. (trans.), *Ibn Fadlan and the Land of Darkness: Arab Travellers in the Far North* (London, 2012)

OTHER USEFUL BOOKS

Barnes, M. P., *Runes A Handbook* (Woodbridge, 2012)
Brink, S. and Price, N. (eds), *The Viking World* (Abingdon, 2008)
Byock, J., *Viking Age Iceland* (London, 2001)
Crossley-Holland, K., *The Penguin Book of Norse Myths: Gods of the Vikings* (London, 2011)
Graham-Campbell, J., *Viking Art* (London, 2013)
Jesch, J., *Viking Poetry of Love and War* (London, 2013)
Jesch, J., *Women in the Viking Age* (Woodbridge, 2001)
McTurk, R. (ed.), *A Companion to Old Norse-Icelandic Literature and Culture* (Oxford, 2007)
Page, R. I., *Chronicles of the Vikings: Records, Memorials and Myths* (London, 2002)
Roesdahl, E., *The Vikings* (London, 1998)
Sawyer, P. (Ed.), *The Oxford Illustrated History of the Vikings* (Oxford, 2001)
Wawn, A., *The Vikings and the Victorians: Inventing the Old North in Nineteenth-Century Britain* (London, 2002)

INTERNET SOURCES

The Icelandic Saga Database includes sagas in both Icelandic and English. (http://sagadb.org/)

The Viking Society for Northern Research has publications about Vikings available for download on its website (http://www.vsnr.org)

The Centre for the Study of the Viking Age at the University of Nottingham provides links to courses, conferences and news items. Follow the CSVA on Twitter @UoNCSVA. (http://www.nottingham.ac.uk/csva)

The World-Tree Project is a digital multimedia archive of resources for teaching and studying the Vikings developed at University College Cork, funded by the IRC New Horizons' scheme. It is a dynamic website where visitors can contribute to the project by submitting items, as well as find out more about the Vikings. It is aimed at all ages and levels of interest. (http:/www. worldtreeproject.org)

FURTHER THINGS TO DO AND SEE

This overview of things to do and see focuses primarily on Britain. The Nordic countries have many more sites than can be listed here.

The British Museum in London has the main display of artefacts in England. The Yorkshire Museum contains a good display of artefacts and The Jorvik Viking Centre recreates a Viking street scene based on the Coppergate excavations. Both are in York. Gosforth, Cumbria, has the Gosforth Cross, the 'fishing stone' and two hogback tombstones at St Mary's Church. Hogback stones can be seen at St Thomas' Church, Brompton, North Yorkshire. It is possible to visit the sites of the battles of Fulford and Stamford Bridge near York. These require imagination to envisage the battles in progress, because of development and changes to the landscape.

The National Museum in Edinburgh has an extensive collection of Viking Age artefacts. Museums at Kirkwall, Orkney, and Lerwick, Shetland, also have displays of Viking Age artefacts. The Brough of Birsay on Orkney was a Viking settlement, and a visit to the tomb at Maeshowe will offer the chance to see Old Norse runic graffiti.

The National Museum of Ireland, Dublin, has an excellent display of Viking Age artefacts.

In Denmark, the National Museum in Copenhagen and museums at Lindholm Høje, Moesgård and Ribe all have good displays. The Roskilde Viking Ship Museum has reconstructed ships and the Skuldelev ships on display. You can also take short tours in reconstructed Viking ships at certain times. The forts at Fyrkat and Trelleborg have reconstructions of the Viking Age sites, while you can climb the grave mounds at Jelling and visit the nearby museum.

In Norway, the Viking Ship Museum in Oslo has the remains of the Gokstad, Oseberg and Tune ships as well as a display of artefacts recovered from them. The Historical Museum in Oslo has the only Viking helmet ever found on display in its Viking gallery. The Lofotr Viking Museum at Borg, Lofoten, includes a reconstructed Viking hall.

Sweden has many runestones to see, so a runic tour is quite possible. The Historiska Museet, Stockholm, and the Lund University Historical Museum have good Viking exhibitions. Birka and Gamla Uppsala are also worth visiting, as is Gotlands Museum for its display of picture stones.

Iceland affords the chance to visit the sites of many of the events described in the sagas. These include Thingvellir, the home of the Viking parliament, Reykholt, where Snorri Sturluson ended his days, and Borg á Mýrum, where Egill Skallagrimsson lived. Perlan in Reykjavik has a saga museum. Árbær Museum has reconstructed houses. The Settlement Exhibition, Aðalstræti 16, Reykjavik, displays an interpretation of the oldest remains of human habitation found in Iceland. The National Museum of Iceland, Reykjavik, contains the main collections.

TRANSLATIONS

PAGE 29: SKALHOLT MAP TRANSLATION

Translation of Latin names:

Mare glaciale: "Ice sea"

Promontorium Winlandiae: "Promontory of Vinland"

Text in panel on map:

Delineation of the northern lands by Sigurd Stefánsson. Year 1570.

Main text:

The author's own explanation of the characters occurring on this map.

A These inhabitants are the ones reached by the English; they derive their name from the dryness, as if torrid and desiccated from the scorching of either the sun or the cold.

B Next to these is Vinland, which they called "the Good" on account of the fecundity of the land and the rich yield of useful things. As our [ancestors] had it, this [land] was bordered by the ocean from the south, but from the narratives of more recent [writers] I gather that it is separated from America by either a strait or a bay.

C They call this the land of Giants because horned Giants reportedly live there; and these they called *Skrickfinna*.

D Are more easterly people who were called *Klofinna* on account of their claws.

E Jotunheim is the same as the land of the more monstrous giants. One may consider the realm of Geirröd and Gudmund to have been located here.

F We understand that here a huge gulf runs out into Russia.

G A rocky region; this one is often mentioned in the history.

H I do not know which island this is, unless it happens to be the one found by that Venetian.

It is maintained that the author of this little geographical table is Sigurd Stefánsson of Iceland, a learned man, once the most worthy rector of the school of Skálholt, who also produced some other specimens of genius and erudition, namely a *Description of Iceland*, which I remember having seen with His Most Serene Majesty's Antiquary, Thormodur Torfason and also a little work on *Spectres*, which, having been communicated to me by a certain friend in my homeland last summer, is kept with me. This map of his, however, seems to have been taken from ancient Icelandic sources. With regard to Helluland, Markland and Skraelingeland, one will be able to consult Arngrim Jonas, who, at the end of his little work on Greenland, noted down some naval expeditions of Greenlanders to these lands. In the delineation of the northern lands beyond Greenland, too, where he places Risaland and Jotunheim, the author has also

followed ancient Icelandic sources, as I know well enough; but I doubt if those are authentic. It is sufficiently established that there is but little agreement between this map and the previous map of His Lordship Gudbrand. Iceland has a width here that is greater than justified; also, the headland of Herjólfsnes has the appearance of a huge mainland rather than an isthmus or a headland – to say nothing of the rest; hence, I have noted down this map for the sake of curiosity rather than because it was necessary.

With thanks to Studiemeesters for the translation.

PAGE 48: ANGLO SAXON CHRONICLE

Translation of first three paragraphs:

A.D. 791.   This year Baldulf was consecrated Bishop of Whitern, on the sixteenth day before the calends of August, by Archbishop Eanbald and Bishop Ethelbert.

A.D. 792.   This year Offa, King of Mercia, commanded that King Ethelbert should be beheaded; and Osred, who had been king of the Northumbrians, returning home after his exile, was apprehended and slain, on the eighteenth day before the calends of October. His body is deposited at Tinemouth. Ethelred this year, on the third day before the calends of October, took unto himself a new wife, whose name was Elfleda.

A.D. 793.   This year came dreadful fore-warnings over the land of the Northumbrians, terrifying the people most woefully: these were immense sheets of light rushing through the air, and whirlwinds, and fiery, dragons flying across the firmament. These tremendous tokens were soon followed by a great famine: and not long after, on the sixth day before the ides of January in the same year, the harrowing inroads of heathen men made lamentable havoc in the church of God in Holy-island, by rapine and slaughter. Siga died on the eighth day before the calends of March.

PAGE 53: LETTER TO ALCUIN TO ETHELRED

[Lo, it is nearly 350 years] that we and our fathers have inhabited this most lovely land, and never before has such terror appeared in Britain as we have now suffered from a pagan race, nor was it thought that such an inroad from the sea could be made. Behold, the church of St Cuthbert spattered with the blood of priests of God, despoiled of all its ornaments; a place more venerable than all in Britain is given as a prey to pagan peoples; And where first, after the departure of St Paulinus from York, the Christian religion in our race took its rise, there misery and calamity have begun. Who does not fear this? Who does not lament this as if his

country were captured? Foxes pillage the chosen vine, the heritage of the Lord has been given to a people not his own; and where there was the praise of God, are now the games of the Gentiles; the holy festivity has been turned to mourning. Consider carefully, brothers, and examine diligently, less perchance this unaccustomed and unheard-of evil was merited by some unheard-of evil practice. I do not say...

PAGE 57: CODEX AUREUS

In the name of our Lord Jesus Christ, I, Earl Alfred, and my wife Werburg procured these books from the heathen invading army with our own money; the purchase was made with pure gold. And we did that for the love of God and for the benefit of our souls, and because neither of us wanted these holy works to remain any longer in heathen hands. And now we wish to present them to Christ Church to God's praise and glory and honour, and as thanksgiving for his sufferings, and for the use of the religious community which glorifies God daily in Christ Church; in order that they should be read aloud every month for Alfred and for Werburg and for Alhthryth, for the eternal salvation of their souls, as long as God decrees that Christianity should survive in that place. And also I, Earl Alfred, and Werburg beg and entreat in the name of Almighty God and of all his saints that no man should be so presumptuous as to give away or remove these holy works from Christ Church as long as Christianity survives there. Alfred Werburg Alhthryth *their daughter*

Sweet's Anglo-Saxon Reader in Prose and Verse, rev. Dorothy Whitelock (Oxford: Clarendon, 1967), p. 205.

PAGES 104–5: THE EDDA OF SNORRI STURLUSON

A translation of this Prologue can be found in any translation of Snorri's *Edda*, see the Further Reading section on page 136.

PAGE 129: THE CODEX REGIUS

This folio contains the last part of *The Death of Sinfiotli* and the beginning of *Gripir's Prophecy*. Translations of these poems can be found in any of the translations of the *Codex Regius* or *Poetic Edda* in the Further Reading section on page 136.

PAGES 132–3: THE FLATEYJARBOK

These pages show the end of the *Saga of Eirik the Far-farer* and the start of the *Saga of Olaf Tryggvason*. English translations of these stories as they are told in this manuscript are not readily available, but a different version of the saga of Olaf Tryggvason can be found in *Heimskringla*, see the Further Reading section on page 136.

INDEX

Page numbers in *italic* type refer to pictures or their captions.

PICTURE CREDITS

MEMORABILIA CREDITS